A TRAVEL GUIDE
TO
BLACK HISTORICAL SITES
AND
LANDMARKS IN NORTH CAROLINA

To Eunice,
for The "Tour Guide and
Historian" in you.
Love,
Bill & Pat *Christmas*
1997

A TRAVEL GUIDE
TO BLACK
HISTORICAL SITES
AND LANDMARKS
IN NORTH CAROLINA

by

Lenwood Davis

Cover Design by Timothy Porter

Winston-Salem, North Carolina

First printing, August, 1991

Library of Congress Catalog Card Number 91-70215
ISBN 1-878177-02-8
Bandit Books, Inc.
P.O. Box 11721
Winston-Salem, NC 27106
919-785-7417

Printed in the United States of America

Dedicated to Phyliss.

ACKNOWLEDGMENTS

Photographs courtesy of:

Lenwood Davis (64, 78, 89, 96, 156, 157, 161, 166, 170, 172, 182)
Fayetteville State University Archives (159)
Jennifer FitzSimons (176)
Winston-Salem Journal (84)
University of North Carolina at Wilmington & New Hanover Museum (151)
Charlotte News and Observer (100)

All other photographs are courtesy of
the North Carolina Division of Archives and History

CONTENTS

PART THREE

INTRODUCTION

More than ten million visitors come to North Carolina every year, and undoubtedly many of them would visit Black historical sites if they knew where such sites were located. This is the first and only guide to Black historical sites and landmarks in North Carolina. This book is designed for the general public, as well as tourists. Moreover, travel agencies, libraries, federal, state and local governments, Chambers of Commerce, Welcome Centers, public schools, as well as researchers and writers will find use for this book. The reader can see and touch the physical evidence of Blacks' contributions and achievements in this state through their monuments, buildings, churches, landmarks, colleges, and highway markers.

Blacks in North Carolina have made significant contributions to the construction and development of this state, yet few people are aware of this fact, because their deeds are seldom recorded in history books. Some local residents, however, have erected permanent monuments and markers to honor Black individuals and their achievements. Hence, future generations can honor their memory. This work serves as a guide to places in North Carolina that testify to the role that Blacks have played in helping to build the Tar Heel State.

This book is divided into three sections. Part One, dealing with historic landmarks and sites, makes up the largest portion of the book. More than one hundred and fifty landmarks and sites are listed. Part Two discusses highway historical markers. It includes forty-six markers. Part Three lists Black restaurants, highlighting their menus, and bookstores. A glossary and index round out this book.

It would have been impossible to include all of the landmarks and sites relating to Black people in North Carolina. Therefore, I have included primarily those listed in the National Register of Historic

Places. While there are many more historical sites, most of them have, over the years, undergone extensive renovations and have not maintained their original structure. Many buildings have been moved from their original site. I used the National Register because it has strict requirements for selection of sites. This register is the official list of the nation's cultural resources worthy of preservation. The National Register of Historic Places is a list of the tangible reminders of the heritage of the United States. It is administered by the National Park Service under the Secretary of the Interior.

The sites used in the National Register are generally nominated by individual states through the State Historical Preservation Officers. The properties, however, must be approved by the Secretary of the Interior before states can nominate historic properties to the National Register. Since it is a great honor to be listed, there are certain standards sites must meet. The National Register's standards for evaluating the significance of properties were developed to recognize the accomplishments of all peoples who have made a contribution to America's history and heritage.

Districts, sites, buildings, structures, and objects which possess integrity of location, design, setting, materials, workmanship, feeling, and association are selected. They must also be significant to American history, architecture, archeology, engineering, and/or culture. The criteria for inclusion of sites are:

1. They are associated with events that have made significant contributions to the broad patterns of our history.
2. They are associated with the lives of people significant in our past.
3. They embody the distinctive characteristics of a type, period, or method of construction, or represent the work of a master, or that possess high artistic values, or that represent a significant and distinguishable

entity whose components may lack individual distinction.
4. They have yielded, or may be likely to yield, information important in prehistory or history.

The North Carolina Department of Cultural Resources administers the Highway Historical Markers Program. Since it cannot mark all historic places in North Carolina, it also has certain criteria that must be met. Unlike the National Register program, anyone is free to submit a proposal for a highway historical marker. There are sixteen criteria. Most of them are general in nature. There are, however, five specific criteria:

1. All markers designate places or persons of statewide significance. No markers will be approved for subjects of purely local or regional importance.
2. No individual can be marked prior to a waiting period of twenty-five years after death.
3. The committee will not single out individuals to mark when many persons have shared equally in an event of historical importance.
4. No structure, whether a house or public building, will be marked merely to preserve it.
5. No marker will be approved for individual sites within an historical complex which has its own marker system.

Of the more than 1,313 state markers erected across North Carolina, only forty-five are related to Black people. The first highway marker to honor Blacks was erected for John Chavis in 1938. The latest, at the time of this publication, was erected in 1991 to honor Anna Cooper and the other Afro-Americans buried in the Raleigh City Cemetery. Joseph Charles Price, the founder of Livingstone

College, minister, orator, and leader, is the only Black to have two markers erected in his honor. One is located in Elizabeth City, his birthplace, and the other is in Salisbury, near where he founded Livingstone College and where he lived.

The Highway Historical Marker Advisory Committee hopes, "for young people, the markers [will] spark a curiosity that leads to further study and appreciation of historical development of the region." The committee notes, "for visitors, the signs may be their only exposure to the history of the Tar Heel State." The committee also wants native North Carolinians to take note of these markers, because they can be a source of pride, "a signal that an event of historical significance took place close to home."

Part Three of this book lists Black restaurants and bookstores. Black restaurants are virtually extinct in North Carolina. Yet, a few have managed to survive. They are included because many of them have special recipes that have been passed down from generation to generation. Visitors to these establishments can taste traditional and "down home" or "soul food" cooking. Most of these restaurants are located in urban areas. Visitors can enjoy tasty meals after visiting the local historical sites.

I include Black bookstores because several of them carry the most complete line of Black books in their area. Furthermore, since there are only a few such bookstores in North Carolina, visitors may want to know where they are located. Many of the bookstores carry not only books, but also other Black products such as greeting cards, records, incense, gifts, games, church materials, clothing, art works, toys, and sorority and fraternity memorabilia. All of these bookstores are located in major metropolitan areas.

Any work of this nature includes the assistance of many people. I would like to thank the staffs of both the North Carolina State Library and the Division of Archives and History for their assistance. I would like to especially thank Michael Hill of the Division of Archives and History for the many suggestions he gave that helped to improve this book. I am indebted to Gloria Powell for sharing with me information that she had on Black historical sites and Black restaurants. I received encouragement for this book from Ralph and Carolyn Black, and James and Betty Gibbs, and I would like to thank them. I also received support and assistance from Phyliss, and I am most appreciative to her. I must thank Kay Marlowe for typing this book and making many helpful suggestions as well as transcribing the handwritten draft to the typed version. I owe a debt of gratitude to my editor, Jennifer Fitz-Simons, for her editorial skills in bringing this work to its fruition. I would also like to thank Gray Erlacher for his many helpful suggestions, as well as Tim Porter for his cover design. And last, but not least, Barry McGee, my publisher, for having the foresight to see the need to publish this book.

Since I hope to revise this volume in the future, I welcome any additions or suggestions from the readers. Send them to:

P.O. Box 11721
Winston-Salem, NC 27106

Editors' Note: The editors wish to thank Ms. Ginny Oswald for last minute help with photography.

Students and faculty of Waters Normal Institute of Winton.
Rev. C.S. Brown is seated.

PART ONE

LANDMARKS

AND

SITES

HISTORICAL
BACKGROUND

It is not clear when Blacks were first present in North Carolina. Some writers of Tar Heel history mention Blacks on the expedition with Hernando De Soto in the 1540s when they supposedly climbed the Blue Ridge Mountains. These same historians suggest that Blacks were also on Juan Pardo's expedition in the 1560s when they marched through the southwestern part of the state.

Slavery, however, was recognized as early as 1665 by the Concessions and Agreement of that year. Four years later, it was given legal status by the Fundamental Constitutions of Carolina drawn up by John Locke, the English political theorist. Article 110 asserted: "Every free man of Carolina, shall have absolute power and authority over his negro slave, of what opinion of religion soever." It also pointed out that any slave converting to Christianity still remained a slave. Because of a shortage of labor supply, the Lords Proprietors had made the offer to "the Owner of every Negro-Man or slave, brought thither to settle within the first year twenty acres, and for every Woman-Negro or slave five acres." The allotments were later increased to fifty acres of land for every slave fourteen years old imported into the colony.

Others have pointed out that Blacks may have come to western North Carolina with the Cherokee Indians as porters and teamsters in the 1670s. The earliest record of Blacks actually being in the colony, however, is 1694, when five Whites claimed extra land for bringing in eight Blacks.

The general population as well as the slave population grew very slowly between 1665 and the early 1700s. In 1712, the total number of Blacks in the colony was estimated to be only about eight hundred. Blacks, both free and enslaved, were in the western part of the state in East Flat Rock, near Asheville, in the 1730s.

By 1767, Blacks who were taxable had increased to twenty-two thousand as compared with twenty-nine thousand Whites who were taxable. North Carolina didn't have a slave population as large as those in South Carolina and Virginia. As late as 1850, seventy-three percent of North Carolina families did not own any slaves. Moreover, only about half the slaveholders owned more than nine. It should be pointed out, however, that about forty to sixty percent of the households in the tobacco-producing areas owned slaves. Slaves not only worked on tobacco plantations, but also on rice plantations and in naval stores industries, such as tar pitch and turpentine. Slaves in colonial North Carolina, like slaves all over the South, were ill-fed, ill-clothed, and poorly housed.

Although there were slaves in prerevolutionary North Carolina, there were also free Blacks. It is not clear when free Blacks first came to North Carolina. The records of 1701 state free Blacks were voting. A complaint was lodged by a group of North Carolinians with the Lords Proprietors of North Carolina in 1705 which makes reference to free Blacks in the Colony in 1701. It states, in part:

> We...humbly represent to your lordships...that it is one of the fundamental Rights and unquestionable privileges to belong to Englishmen that all elections of their Representatives to serve in Parliament ought to be free and indifferent and that no alien born out of allegiance to the Crown of England...ought to elect for, or be elected to serve as a member of assembly.

But in 1701, the votes of many unqualified aliens were taken. The votes of several free Blacks were also taken.

Because of the increasing existence of free Blacks in the colony, the Colonial Assembly began to enact laws to deny suffrage to free Blacks. The colony passed the first Black codes in 1715, preventing free Blacks from voting and marrying Whites. The codes also regulated the activities of servants and slaves. Slaves could not leave their plantations without a ticket or a White servant with them, nor could slaves gather to worship. A number of codes were passed in 1723, 1741, 1753, and 1758. Each law increasingly regulated every aspect of the lives of both free Blacks and slaves. Although laws governing their activities were on the statute books, Blacks did not always obey them because the laws were often inconsistent and ambiguous.

In North Carolina, free Blacks served in the military until the 19th century, and although the 1715 law disallowed free Blacks to vote, the King of England repealed the statute in 1737, because it permitted other free men as well as freeholders to vote. The North Carolina Constitution of 1776 made no racial distinction for suffrage. Free Blacks in North Carolina voted until they were disenfranchised in 1835.

Even before the American Revolution, there were numerous instances of slaves in North Carolina rebelling and running away. It was the American Revolution, however, that saw the largest number of slaves rebelling by joining the British Army. In 1775, Lord Dunmore of England promised freedom to all slaves who would enlist, encouraging hundreds to flee. After 1775, George Washington moved to enlist free Blacks to prevent them from joining the British side. The problem of defending North Carolina became so acute that the 1779 Assembly offered freedom to all slaves who served in the army. At no time, however, if the records are accurate, did large numbers of Blacks of North Carolina serve in the Revolutionary Army. In the general division of the army under Washington in 1778, there were at least seventy Black men in the North Carolina Brigade. Most, if not all, were free Blacks.

Black North Carolinians have supported the state and country in every war from the American Revolution to the war with Iraq, and have been as patriotic as any other ethnic group.

The religious life of the Black people in North Carolina was one of self-help, necessity, good will, and determination. From their beginnings in the 1830s until today, churches have provided firm support for Blacks. Almost all Black churches share the same origins--they came into existence from free African churches begun before the Civil War from Southern Protestant branches, and from Northern missionary efforts in the 1880s. In several instances, Blacks established churches because they were not fully accepted in the White churches. In a number of cases, Whites helped Blacks establish churches of their own. To Black people, the church was an extension of their home. It was more than a place of worship; it also served as a meeting place, a recreation facility, a comforter, and a nursery.

Over the years, Black North Carolinians have served as leaders, town commissioners, politicians, school board members, educators, ministers, physicians, college presidents, businessmen, soldiers, policemen, and a host of other things too numerous to mention. Their contributions are due not only to noteworthy achievement, but also to steadfast and quiet determination. Blacks worked hard, believed in family life, and had compassion for their less fortunate neighbors. The acknowledgment of Black achievements is long overdue. It is hoped that this work will, in some small way, draw attention to Black people's contribution to their local communities, cities, state, and the nation as a whole.

NORTHEAST REGION

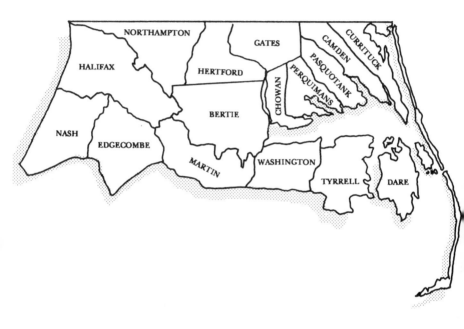

Creswell	New Hope Township
Edenton	Newland Township
Elizabeth City	Nixonton Township
Hamilton	Parkville Township
Hertford	Tarboro
Manteo	Winfall

CRESWELL

Somerset Place

Somerset Place is a plantation, built in 1830 by Josiah Collins III on the shores of Lake Phelps in Pettigrew State Park. It was one of the largest in the state. Although most North Carolinians never owned slaves–in 1860, less than one percent of Whites held over fifty Blacks–Josiah had many. He was one of only four planters in the state with more than three hundred slaves. Most Somerset Place Blacks are descendants of slaves who were purchased by Josiah Collins near Edenton in the 1780s and who adopted the surname "Collins," although there were about twenty different families in the Somerset Black population.

The White Collins family kept meticulous records of slave births, deaths, marriages, health, ages, and skills. The accounts reveal that Blacks maintained fairly cohesive families. Some of the slaves were literate. Blacks earned money by raising vegetables and selling their services to other farmers. They purchased nice clothing and fancy jewelry at a plantation store. Christmas at Somerset was renowned throughout eastern North Carolina for lavish banquets, music recitals, and poetry readings, as well as the joyous slave celebration known as "John Kooner," which originated in Africa and the Caribbean. Blacks built the "Big House" slave quarters and hospital, and they dug a six-mile long canal.

Most of the historical background information for this sketch was taken from the pamphlet "Somerset Place." This is a North Carolina historic site administered by the Division of Archives and History. From *April l through October 31, hours are: Monday - Saturday, 9:00 a.m. to 5:00 p.m., Sunday, l:00 p.m. to 5:00 p.m.; November l through March 31, Tuesday - Saturday, 10:00 a.m. to 4:00 p.m., Sunday, 1:00 p.m. to 4:00 p.m.*

It is closed on Monday. This site is located on **NC 64 nine miles south of Creswell.** Phone (919) 797-4560. ADMISSION IS FREE.

EDENTON

St. John's Church

St. John's Church

The parish of St. John the Evangelist Episcopal Church began April 6, 1881, as a mission station. It was composed of members transferred from several churches in the area. The diocese had provided a great deal of support for the church, and a good friend of the new congregation had already built a structure. Consecrated the day the parish was formed, this building was demolished by a tornado on July 26, 1884. Enough of the structure remained, however, to provide the framework for a new building for which the cornerstone was laid July 8, 1885. The new church was consecrated May 22, 1887.

It has since been widened on both sides and a sacristy now connects it to the parish house.

In 1888, W. J. Herritage, as lay reader, began many years of service including his own ordination work in neighboring towns and the beginning of a parochial school in 1892. The present parish house was apparently the second school building, completed in 1902. During the thirty years before county schools existed, St. John's provided invaluable educational service to the community, especially after the arrival of the Rev. S. N. Griffith in 1920. After commencement, 1931, the school was discontinued at that location and merged with the county system.

The marble font given by Philadelphia churchmen to the first church, though damaged, is still functional. The original parish register, beginning April 6, 1881, has survived in good condition. The historical information was supplied by the church, which is located on **East Church Street.**

ELIZABETH CITY

Elizabeth City State University

Although Elizabeth City State University was formed in 1891, none of its original buildings still stand. There are, however, several buildings which were erected in the early 1900s. Located **on the campus at Parkview Drive,** they are as follows:

Lane Hall was erected in 1909 and is believed to be the oldest building on campus. Named for Frances Lane Bias (1895-1980), wife of the second president, this one-story building once housed all of the academic and administrative operations on campus. It has been renovated several times. It is presently used for geological sciences and other offices.

McLendon Hall, erected in 1920, is the second oldest building on campus. This structure, formerly known as the "ARK," was once a schoolhouse. It was named for Lucille M. McLendon, former teacher-training supervisor. It has housed various operations and has been renovated several times since its construction. The building is presently used by the Early Childhood Education Center and ROTC.

Moore Hall, probably the third oldest building on campus, was erected in 1922. In 1939, with funds from the Federal Works Agency of the Public Works Administration (PWA), an addition was built. This two-story structure was named in honor of Peter Weddick Moore (1859-1934), first president of the university. It has been renovated several times and has housed many classrooms and offices. It presently contains academic and administrative offices.

Built in 1926, **Butler Hall** is the fourth oldest structure on campus. It was named for John Henry Manning Butler, the second teacher at the school, who died in 1944. This three-story building serves as a men's residence hall.

Mount Lebanon A.M.E. Zion Church

Mount Lebanon African Methodist Episcopal (A.M.E.) Zion Church was built in 1855 by several Black citizens who wanted to spread Zionism in the northeastern part of North Carolina. Although the congregation was small, it subsequently grew and needed larger quarters. The present brick church was built in 1905. The church is located on **Clupper Street.**

Olive Branch Baptist Church

Olive Branch Baptist Church was organized in 1866. Before then, during the time of slavery, Blacks had been attending First Baptist Church, which was for Whites. After emancipation, however, Blacks wanted their own church, and with the help of Whites in the city, they built Olive Branch Baptist Church. This Gothic Revival-style building with its tower is thought to be one of the oldest Black churches in the city in continuous use. Olive Branch Baptist Church has been a source of spiritual and social uplift for the Black community for over 125 years. The church is located at **510 Brooks Avenue.**

Cornerstone Missionary Baptist Church

Cornerstone Missionary Baptist Church was erected in 1888 as an outgrowth of Olive Branch Baptist Church. Several members became dissatisfied with conditions at Olive Branch, and left to form Cornerstone Missionary. This church has been a positive influence in the community for over one hundred years, and continues to work for better and improved race relations in the city. This Gothic Revival building with its tower is located at **505 South Main Street.**

HAMILTON

Rosenwald Colored School

The Rosenwald Colored School was built in Hamilton in 1914. Julius Rosenwald, president of Sears & Roebuck of Chicago, provided funds that were matched locally by either private or public financing for more than five thousand Black schools in fifteen states. This was the first "Rosenwald" school in Martin County and functioned until 1960 when a new school was opened. The new brick structure was named for Edna Andrews, a former teacher of the "Rosenwald" school. The old school, originally located on Main Street near the Sycamore Baptist Church, is the only remaining structure of early Black schools in Martin County. The wooden building, with its original four windows flanking the entrance door, is located on the **southside of Waldo Street and is the last structure before the Roanoke River in Hamilton.**

Sycamore Baptist Church

The exact year of the founding of Sycamore Baptist Church has not been conclusively determined; however, it appears to have been built between 1880 and 1890. The earliest known place of worship was a bush arbor on the site of the present church which was built about 1900. In 1905, there were about three hundred members in its congregation. This church was the center of religious and social life for nearby farms and towns, such as Oak City and Goose Nest. Sycamore Baptist Church had a very active Sunday School and was

Sycamore Baptist Church

well-attended. Reverend Willis Outterbridge was the pastor in 1890, after whom Reverend A. Cooper served as pastor beginning in 1896. Lancet windows with colored panes and the Colonial Revival entrance doors were added in 1970 during remodeling of this vernacular frame church. The church is located on **northside Main Street beside the Roanoke River in Hamilton.**

HERTFORD

Edy Wood House

The Edy Wood House was built ca. 1832. This one-story, coastal cottage is believed to have been built for Edy Wood, a free Black woman who owned the property in 1832. In 1881 it was sold to Josiah Elliott, a Baptist minister. The house has a center hall plan; two chimneys laid in one to five common bond; and Greek Revival details. This house is probably the oldest existing Black-owned home in Perquimans County. Some of the historic data for this house was taken from the "Hertford Historic Walking Tour." The house is located at **128 West Grubb Street.**

MANTEO

The Black Lifesavers and Coast Guardsmen Memorial

The Black Lifesavers and Coast Guardsmen Memorial was recently erected to honor the only all-Black unit of the Coast Guard at the Pea Island Lifesaving Station. The memorial is a four-foot high, granite marker with a bronze plaque containing the inscription: "To the crews of Pea Island who risked their lives and endured so that others might live." The memorial is located at **the North Carolina Aquarium in Manteo**. The memorial was placed at the aquarium because Richard Etheridge, the first Black to serve as officer in charge of the station, is buried on the aquarium grounds. Pea Island is the northern portion of Hatteras Island.

Black crewmen manned the Pea Island station for nearly seventy years, from 1880 until 1947 when the station was decommissioned. Before Blacks served on Pea Island, they were usually given either cooking or animal-care duties. Few Blacks were surfmen. Tradition has it that this all-Black unit established a reputation for heroism and carved out a niche in history. Another report declared that the Black crew members were treated well by the White community and even permitted to attend the White churches and movie theaters. Mr. Rhett B. White, director of the aquarium, best summed up the significance of this memorial when he said, "The marker will provide a glimpse of Black contributions to lifesaving lore for half a million visitors each year."

NEW HOPE TOWNSHIP

Galatia Baptist Church

Galatia Baptist Church was built in the 1870s. Although the present wooden structure has been modified over the years, it still maintains some of its originality. The church has Gothic lancet-arch, stained-glass windows and doorways and an old bell mounted on a stand in front. It has been well-kept over its 120 year history. This church has played a significant role in the lives of Black people in New Hope for many years. It is located **off of New Hope Road.**

Leigh's Temple A.M.E. Zion Church

Leigh's Temple A.M.E. Zion Church was built in the 1890s. This structure has been modified several times since then. It does, however, maintain some of its originality. The church has Gothic lancet-arch, stained-glass windows, and steeple. It has played a valuable role in the spiritual and social life of the Black community over the years. The church is located **off of New Hope Road.**

Oak Hill A.M.E. Zion Church

Oak Hill A.M.E. Zion Church was erected in the late 1800s. This Gothic structure, with its double-leaf door entrance and bell tower, stands between a former one-room schoolhouse and a small cemetery. This well-preserved edifice has provided spiritual support for Blacks in the New Hope community for nearly one hundred years. The church is located **east of New Hope Road.**

NEWLAND TOWNSHIP

Carver Slave House

The Carver Slave House is reported to be Pasquotank County's only former slave house. This two-room structure was one of six slave houses owned by Job Carver and was reportedly built in the 1850s. This building is now part of the Carver-Etheridge-Gregory Farm. The farm is located on **SR 1360 in Newland Township.**

NIXONTON TOWNSHIP

Pitts Chapel A.M.E. Zion Church

Pitts Chapel A.M.E. Zion Church was built in 1890. This wooden structure has Gothic arched stained-glass windows and a pointed bell tower with three tiers of openings. Much of this church's interior is unaltered. The sanctuary is well-preserved and has been instrumental in the spiritual and social development of the Nixonton Township Black community in its more than one hundred year history. The church is located on **SR 1169 in Nixonton Township.**

PARKVILLE TOWNSHIP

Porter's Chapel A.M.E. Zion Church

Porter's Chapel A.M.E. Zion Church was built in the late 1800s but retains much of its original character. Its steeple, with enclosed bell tower, is representative of church architecture in the late 1800s. The church has semi-Gothic-style, lancet windows, and a tall distinctive belfry. The two-room Fork Bridge School is adjacent to the church. This former school is badly in need of repair. The church is located **in Parkville Township.**

TARBORO

St. Paul Baptist Church

St. Paul Baptist Church was organized in 1871 with sixteen members from the Black community. George C. Caine, a Virginia native, led the church. He settled in Tarboro with his wife, Agnes, soon after the Civil War ended. They initiated a weekly prayer service because of the lack of Black churches in the community. Within a few years, the new church was established under the leadership of Reverend S. A. Davis, who was assisted by A. F. Flood, Samuel Perry, and Reverend Thomas Owens, the latter, a minister of the White Baptist church.

The church building was moved from its Main Street site to the present location ca. 1926. The church's windows occur singly and in trios, with tiny outlining panes typical of the Queen Anne style. The wall surfaces are weatherboarded and enriched with bands of panels, brackets, labels over windows, and other ornamentation, all beautifully preserved. Unfortunately the corner tower, which originally rose to a dramatic, multi-gabled belfry, has been awkwardly truncated in recent years (ca. 1976) and replaced with a reduced upper level. Otherwise, the church is unaltered. Inside

St. Paul Baptist Church

the dominant space is a large open sanctuary under a dome with an oculus. Most of the original woodwork, typical of the turn of the century, is intact. Reflecting the circular orientation created by the dome are the curved pews, a notable and important remnant of the period. St. Paul Baptist Church is one of the most important properties in the Tarboro Historic District and has played a vital role in the spiritual and social life of the Black Tarboro community for more than 120 years. The church is located on the **northwest corner of Edmondson Street at Lloyd Street in Tarboro.**

WINFALL

Popular Run A.M.E. Zion Church

Popular Run A.M.E. Zion Church, organized before 1873, is the oldest Black church in Winfall, and perhaps in Perquimans County. The church has two bell towers, lancet windows, and a three-bay gabled front. This picturesque church has served the spiritual and social needs of the Black community of the town of Winfall for more than 115 years. The church is located **near NC 37 in Winfall.**

CENTRAL COASTAL REGION

Beaufort
Kinston
Selma
Wilson

BEAUFORT

Purvis Chapel

Purvis Chapel

Purvis Chapel was founded in 1820, according to a Beaufort Historical Association marker, by the Methodists in the town. Both Blacks and Whites attended it. It was named after James Purvis, who had held a great revival there. In 1863, Purvis Chapel apparently left the White Methodist Conference and became a member of the African Methodist Episcopal Zion Church Conference. Thus, the church was renamed Purvis Chapel A.M.E. Zion Church. The wooden structure has undergone few modifications over its 170 year history. The church has pointed, stained-glass windows, a double-door central entrance, a porch with two columns, boxed pews, a boxed-cornice pediment, and a gable ornament. Purvis Chapel is the oldest Black church in Carteret County and has been the center of the social and spiritual development for the Black community of Beaufort for many years. The church is located **off of NC 70 at the corner of Broad and Craven Streets.**

KINSTON

Peoples Bank Building

The Peoples Bank Building was constructed about 1923 on Bright Street. The early founders and subscribers of this Black bank included T. B. Holloway, a grocer; C. H. Bynum, a physician; and J. G. Banton, a barber. The bank had capital stock worth about $25,000. The objectives of the company, according to the Record of Corporations, were as follows:

(1) To conduct a commercial banking business;
(2) To conduct a savings banking business;
(3) To do a general trust business in all its phases, and
    to have all the power incident thereto;
(4) To act as fiscal agent, factor, executor, administrator
    or trustee for any person, firm or corporations upon
    such terms as may be agreed upon.

After several years, the bank became so successful that it had to move to a larger building. The bankers built a two-story, Classical Revival building on the corner of South Queen and East Bright Streets. During the Great Depression, Peoples, like many other banks, suffered financially and went out of business.

Peoples Bank was at one time one of the most architecturally sophisticated structures in Kinston's thriving Black commercial district. Even today, this flat-roofed building, with its raised parapet,

The former Peoples Bank Building

ornamented brick panels outlined in limestone, and diamond-shaped, stone bosses, is still a significant structure in this commercial district, now undergoing a regeneration with government assistance.

Over the years various businesses have occupied the former Peoples Bank Building. Some of these businesses include: a dry cleaning business, dentist's office, insurance office, attorney's office, and barber shop. The building is presently occupied by Hairy's Style Shop and is located at **242 South Queen Street.**

SELMA

St. John's A.M.E. Church Parsonage

The St. John's African Methodist Episcopal Church Parsonage was built in 1926 while Reverend W. H. Hall was serving as pastor. The church itself was built in 1898 but the original building was destroyed by fire. Reverend Hall lived in the two and one-half-story frame house for several years. The house is a modest, hip-roofed bungalow with a wide front porch. The two-bay elevation has a central, hip-roofed dormer and paired second-story windows. It also has an unusual projecting bay window on one side. It is located at **402 South Sumner Street.** *(PRIVATE RESIDENCE)*

W. S. King House

The W. S. King House is a two-story frame house, built around 1900 by W. S. King, who was principal of the local Black school for many years. (W. S. King School in Morehead City, North Carolina, was named after the educator.) The house is a square, hip-roofed structure with projecting front and side gabled bays. The front projection has chamfered corners, a porch, and a three-bay, front elevation entrance at the center of the facade. The home is located at **212 West Watson Street.** *(PRIVATE RESIDENCE)*

WILSON

East Wilson has long been identified with the Black community. The buildings in the community include homes, churches, schools, hospitals, and commercial structures, some of which were built between 1880 and 1930. Because of urban renewal and redevelopment, several buildings have been torn down. The city of Wilson has started a renovation and rehabilitation program to preserve many of these structures . The following buildings are examples of significant historic landmarks:

Mercy Hospital, built ca. 1913, was one of the earliest hospitals for Blacks in the state. The hospital operated until its closing in 1929. It reopened in 1930 and continued to operate until it closed again in 1964. This structure, in Classical Revival style, with Doric portico, and a three-bay facade sheltered by a two-story portico, was sold to Calvary United Presbyterian Church in 1964. The church leased the building to the Wilson Community Improvement Association. The building is presently being renovated and is located at **504 East Green Street.**

The S. H. Vick House is the most imposing residence in East Wilson. This house was built for S. H. Vick ca. 1904. Although this Tudor-style, towered house has undergone extensive renovation, it remains impressive. S. H. Vick was principal of the Wilson Grade School. At one time or another, Vick also served as Wilson's postmaster, missionary, real estate agent, hotel owner, banker, and businessman. This house is located at **622 East Green Street.**

The Halley B. Taylor House was built around 1913 for Reverend Taylor, who was pastor of Calvary Presbyterian Church. The house has an L-plan influenced by the Colonial Revival style. It also has a Palladian window and a large wraparound porch. The house is located at **721 East Green Street.**

St. John's African Methodist Episcopal Zion Church was built in 1915 by brickmason, John Barnes. The church is an example of the Gothic Revival style with its corner tower; stained-glass, arched windows; and slate roof. This church is located at **119 North Pender Street.**

The Camillus L. Darden House was built ca. 1925 by Camillus L. Darden, the son of Charles H. Darden, who was reported to have been the first Black undertaker in North Carolina. Camillus and his brother, Arthur, later took over their father's mortuary business. His brother-in-law, John Barnes, the brickmason mentioned above, built this Colonial Revival-style home. This two-story house also exhibits elements of the Mission Revival style. The house is located at **108 North Pender Street.**

The Oliver Nestus Freeman House was built ca. 1910. Mr. Freeman graduated from Tuskegee Institute with a degree in industrial arts. He designed and built this bungalow-style house. Mr. Freeman later covered the cottage with rough-stone masonry. The house has a mock, half-timbered shed dormer and rough-stone masonry porch columns. Mr. Freeman was apparently known in Wilson for the whimsical masonry sculpture garden at his home. The house is located at **1300 East Nash Street.**

The Dr. Frank S. Hargrave House is next door to the S. H. Vick House and is also impressive. Built for Dr. Hargrave around 1920, it is an example of the Colonial Revival style. Dr. Hargrave received a medical degree from Shaw University and practiced medicine in Wilson from 1913 to 1923. He was also director of Mercy Hospital during this time. In 1924, Dr. Hargrave moved to Orange, New Jersey. Although this house has undergone extensive renovation, its original style is apparent. This house is located at **624 East Green Street.**

The Hardy Johnson House is different in style from the Vick and Hargrave homes. The Johnson house was built much earlier, ca. 1901, and resembles Queen Anne-style architecture with some aspects of the Colonial Revival style. Hardy Johnson was a fireman for a number of years. This two-story house is well-preserved and has a cross-gable wing to one side with a two-story, faceted bay. The house is located at **705 East Green Street.**

The Ada Winstead House was built for Miss Winstead, a seamstress, between 1922 and 1925. This two-story house has a hip-roofed balcony with a latticed balustrade on top of a wide front porch. This house is located at **415 East Green Street.**

The Short W. Barnes House was reportedly built ca. 1921 by Mr. Barnes, who worked as a carpenter. The house is a classic bungalow with a dormer balcony. The structure also has an open, semi-circular side porch off the three-sided bay. This house is located at **616 East Green Street.**

Shotgun-Style Houses

Shotgun-style houses were built around 1925 for Black workers, such as drivers, porters, and cooks. These particular houses are very

distinctive because they include a row of identical houses completely
intact. All have had extensive renovation, nonetheless, such architecture is rare today. These houses also are a reflection of the Bungalow
style of the late 1920s. They are located at **806-814 East Green Street.**

The Charles H. Darden High School

The Charles H. Darden High School was built in 1923 and named
in honor of Mr. Darden, who was the state's first Black undertaker.
This two-story school was built in Tudor style. This building has an
Art Deco doorway with brick pilasters dividing the facade into seven
distinct parts. The school is located at **504 North Carroll Street.**

CAPE FEAR REGION

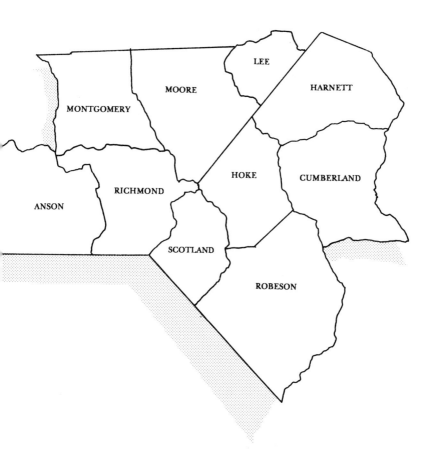

LEE

MOORE

HARNETT

MONTGOMERY

HOKE

CUMBERLAND

ANSON

RICHMOND

SCOTLAND

ROBESON

Wilmington

WILMINGTON

Chestnut Street United Presbyterian Church

The Chestnut Street United Presbyterian Church is the result of an inspired elder of First Presbyterian Church who attended an elders and deacons convention in Greensboro. When he returned to Wilmington he started prayer meetings at First Presbyterian. Within three months forty-two Whites and twenty Blacks were received into the communion of the church. The congregation of First Presbyterian also erected a mission chapel on Chestnut Street between Seventh and Eighth Streets in 1858 as a thanks offering for God's mercy. On November 6, 1858, fourteen of the Black people, dissatisfied with First Presbyterian, left to form the Second Presbyterian Church. The new church was organized by the Presbytery of Fayetteville. The Reverend Martin McQueen became its first minister, serving from 1859 until 1863. The congregation of Second Presbyterian worshipped from its inception until 1867 in the structure originally erected by the First Presbyterian Church as a mission chapel on Chestnut Street.

On October 8, 1866, a committee of the Second Presbyterian Church, consisting of Messrs. Alexander Sprunt, John A. Taylor, and John C. Latta were authorized by the church to sell the Chestnut Street property to the trustees of the First African Presbyterian Church of Wilmington. The trustees were William Cutlar, Henry Taylor, Elvin Artis, Duncan Haynes, Alfred Hargrave, Owen Burney, David Sadgwar, Edward Davis, Sandy Howe, Alice Price, and James Cutlar. The sale was final in 1867. The Second Church thereafter worshipped in Brooklyn Hall.

The First African Presbyterian Church on Chestnut Street is basically the same. A choir room was added to the back of the building and the porch was removed from the front.

The Reverend Peter Hodges (1866-1868) believed, like the Pilgrims, that church and school should go hand in hand; that children should be taught to study the Word of God. In accordance with this, a parochial school was organized.

The work continued to grow for years under succeeding ministers. A manse was built. The congregation produced various avocations: School principals, teachers, General Assembly representatives, a missionary to Africa, and the town's first Black doctor.

Over the past thirteen years, the old furniture in the sanctuary has been replaced with new. The interior has been redecorated and the exterior painted. Central heating and air conditioning were installed. A multi-purpose building adjoining the sanctuary was erected in 1967, where the church school, Christian Education projects, and fellowship hours are now held. The church is well equipped to offer a service to the community and willingly accepts the challenge. The historical background of this 133 year old edifice was supplied by the church. The church is located at **710-1/2 Chestnut Street.**

SOUTHERN PIEDMONT REGION

SAMPSON

DUPLIN

BLADEN

PENDER

COLUMBUS

NEW HANOVER

BRUNSWICK

Fayetteville

FAYETTEVILLE

Orange Street School

The Orange Street School is believed to be the oldest public education structure of either the White or Black race remaining in Fayetteville. The two-story brick building with Neo-Classical detailing was built ca. 1915 as an elementary school by a locally prominent Black contractor, James Waddell. In 1927, a high school, which eventually became E. E. Smith High School, was opened on the second floor of the building, with the elementary school remaining on the first floor. During this time, the high school was one of only two such Black institutions in Cumberland County. The high school was moved out of the building in 1929 but returned in 1931.

The Orange Street School Building

E. E. Smith High School moved to newer quarters in 1940. The Orange Street School remained an elementary school until 1951. In that year it became a junior high school, thus marking the first time since its opening that it did not house an elementary school. In 1953, the junior high was removed and the building was used by the Board of Education for offices and storage until 1983, when it was abandoned. In 1986, the Cumberland County Board of Education deeded the building to the Orange Street School Restoration and Historic Association, Inc., for one dollar. Its plans to restore the building as a museum of public education have drawn wide support in the area. The school is an important symbol of the improvements made in Black public education in Fayetteville during the first half of the century. The building is located at **311 West Orange Street.**

Evans Metropolitan
A.M.E. Zion Church

The history of the Evans Metropolitan A.M.E. Zion Church is directly linked to the establishment of the first Methodist Church in Fayetteville ca. 1800. Situated on Cool Spring Street, the church still occupies the site of the original Methodist Church which was founded by the free Black Virginia shoemaker-preacher, Henry Evans. A free Black founding a church which served both Black and White members was unique in early nineteenth century North Carolina denominational history. After the establishment of the predominantly White Hay Street Methodist Episcopal Church in the early 1830s, the Cool Spring church continued to be favored by Black worshippers and by the 1870s became part of the African Methodist Episcopal Zion Church in its own right, becoming the focus of the Black community after emancipation. Evans Church occupied an important place among Fayetteville churches. The present-day brick edifice was con-

Evans Metropolitan A.M.E. Zion Church

structed between 1893 and 1894. The fourth church to stand on the site, this building is a notable example of the revived Gothic style and testifies to the skill of Black artisans James Williams and Joseph Steward. It features two-story, gable-front brick construction, double-front towers, stained-glass, lancet windows, and notable beaded woodwork inside. The church is located at **301 North Cool Street.**

St. Joseph's Episcopal Church

St. Joseph's Episcopal Church in Fayetteville is comprised of closely grouped buildings, with the chapel, parish hall, and a parsonage linked by wooden arcades. St. Joseph's was built in 1896 to serve a Black congregation which had formed in 1873. It is the second oldest Episcopal congregation in Fayetteville. When a 1916 fire destroyed all but the church, the complex was soon rebuilt in a style which complemented the chapel. The buildings were executed in the shingled Queen Anne style, with sophistication unusual in the region. Bold and organic, green-shingled forms are accented by touches of the English, Gothic, and Spanish styles. One of the most architecturally significant complexes in Fayetteville, this is a rare and valuable survival of the period of American architecture when a close-knit group of structures was arranged and landscaped to give the character of a small country village. The church is located on **Moore Street.**

St. Joseph's Episcopal Church

TRIANGLE REGION

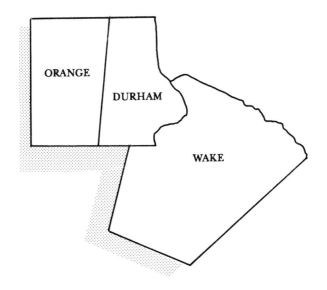

Durham
Hillsborough
Raleigh

DURHAM

North Carolina Central University

North Carolina Central University was founded in 1910 by James E. Shepard as the National Religious Training School. Although none of the institution's original buildings still stand, several are listed on the National Register of Historic Places. The buildings are located on the campus in **the 1800-1900 blocks of Fayetteville Street.** They include the following buildings:

The **B. N. Duke Auditorium** on campus was completed in 1937 as part of the Public Works Administration (PWA) building campaign. The focal point of the flat-roofed building, with English bond elevations, is the two-story, wooden portico supported by streamlined Corinthian columns. The portico shelters the three identical entrances, each containing double doors and a transom with muntins in a lattice of pointed arches, and a denticulated cornice. A curved, Georgian entablature tops the surround. The auditorium seats nine hundred and is named in honor of one of the school's major benefactors, whose contributions and bequests total approximately $125,000.

The **(Former) President's House** is located at **1902 Fayetteville Street.** In 1923, trustee J. B. Mason, president of Citizen's Bank in Durham, headed a fund drive to construct a new home for the school's president, James E. Shepard. Prior to this time, Shepard lived in a small frame house on the campus. Both Black and White citizens of Durham contributed to the building campaign. In 1925, this two-story house with a brick facade was completed.

The **Clyde R. Hoey Administration Building** is located on campus. Completed in 1929, it is the centerpiece of North Carolina Central University and its most architecturally distinctive building. Atwood and Nash designed three buildings which comprised the late 1920s building campaign heralding the school's charter as North Carolina College. Hoey is one of them. The building is three stories high, with a basement elevated in the rear due to the topography of the site. It features Flemish bond elevations, and the heaviest application of limestone on any of the campus buildings. There are quoins on each of the end-entrance pavilions and smooth-faced blocks sheathing the first story and basement, all in limestone.

Annie Day Shepard Hall is located on campus. This three-story, women's dormitory designed by Atwood and Nash was completed in 1930. It resembles the Clyde R. Hoey Administration Building in its long, hip-roofed form with end pavilions, as well as a gabled entrance pavilion. Here, however, the quoins are brick. Only the string course at the base of the third story and the keystones in the flat splayed brick lintels are limestone. Annie Day Shepard was the wife of the school's founder and the granddaughter of noted North Carolina furniture maker, Thomas Day.

The **Alexander Dunn Building** on campus is a one-story structure in the Georgian Revival style. Also designed by Atwood and Nash, it was completed in 1930 and served as the dining hall for the new college campus. Originally T-shaped, two wings have since been added to the rear so that it is now almost square. Capped by a truncated hip roof, the Flemish bond elevations feature rectangular windows topped with flat wooden lunettes set in arched brick lintels.

The **Albert Lewis Turner Hall** is located on campus. Completed in December 1937, this tall T-shaped and hip-roofed, one-story building, with mezzanine and raised basement, is a product of the campus building campaign sponsored by the Public Works Administration. Tall windows, with splayed brick lintels and limestone keystones, punctuate brick elevations in English bond. The building's interior, the most elegant of the entire campus, has a foyer leading to an oval lobby, with chair rails and wainscotting featuring apnels outlined in applied molding. Constructed as a library, the building later served as the law school and today contains offices. The building was named for a former dean of the undergraduate school.

The **Ruth G. Rush Hall** on campus is a women's dormitory named for a long-time Dean of Women. Completed in 1939, the Georgian Revival-style building was also part of the school's Public Works Administration sponsored campus building campaign.

The **William H. Robinson Science Building** is located on campus. Built in 1939, this three-story, brick building with raised basement was designed by government architect, John M. Carmody, for the Public Works Administration, which funded its construction. It was named in honor of a physics professor who taught at the school from 1937 to 1962.

The **James S. Lee Biology Building** on campus was built in 1956. This Georgian Revival building is thoroughly compatible with the older campus buildings. It is also a rectangular, three-story structure with a raised basement, hip-roofed form, and English bond walls. Cast limestone appears only at the entrances; those at the ends of the building have surrounds with Tuscan half-columns. The main entrance features a convex, one-story portico supported by four Tuscan columns.

Angus W. McLean Dormitory is located on campus. This dormitory, also constructed as part of the Public Works Administration building program in 1937, is identical in form to Shepard Hall except that it lacks the shallow end pavilions. Some distinguishing details include a molded box-cornice with medallions and a main entrance distinguished by a wooden surround with fluted pilasters, entablature, and flat denticulated cornice. Named in honor of the North Carolina governor instrumental in arranging state appropriations of $100,000 for new brick buildings.

Besides the buildings on campus, there is also the **NCCU Art Museum**. The museum contains paintings, sculptures, prints, African Art, and artifacts. Some of the artists' work on display include: Romare Bearden, Jacob Lawrence, Richmond Barthe, Hale Woodruff, Edward M. Bannister, Elizabeth Catlett, Charles White, Selma Burke, Robert S. Duncanson, Ernie Barnes, Edward Wilson, Geoffrey Holder, and Richard Hunt. The museum also has art works from the local public school students. It is located **next to the Music and Art Buildings.** The museum is *open Tuesday-Friday, 9:00 a.m.-5:00 p.m., and 2:00 p.m.-5:00 p.m., Sunday. Closed Saturday and Monday.*

North Carolina Mutual Life Insurance Building

Although the present North Carolina Mutual Life Insurance Building was built in 1966, it is considered an historic site because of its significance to the city of Durham, the state of North Carolina, and the United States. The building was reported to be the nation's first prestressed and postensioned, concrete high rise. It was designed by Welton Becket and Associates and has attracted international attention, receiving a number of architectural design awards. This insurance company is the largest Black-managed financial institution in the world. In keeping with its tradition of being one of the cornerstones of Black capitalism in America, it has a Black Heritage

Room in its building. The building is located at **Duke and West Chapel Hill Streets.**

Stagville Center

The Bennehan-Cameron family owned one of the largest North Carolina plantations in the pre-Civil War South. Approximately nine hundred slaves worked that land, which totalled almost thirty thousand acres by 1860. Stagville, a plantation of several thousand acres, lay at the center of this enormous estate. By the end of the 18th century, the plantation form of agriculture had taken root here as well. Richard Bennehan, a transplanted Virginia merchant, ran the plantation. By 1800, he ranked among the region's largest planters,

Structures on Stagville Plantation

owning four thousand acres and forty slaves who raised tobacco, grain, and livestock for market.

The slave community grew in size as well. Rows of slave houses stood on both the Bennehan and Cameron-owned plantations. The Horton Grove quarter housed perhaps eighty men, women, and children in its two-story, four-room houses. Four surviving slave houses can be seen at the Stagville Center, as well as a large barn (thirty-five by thirty-three feet), built by the highly skilled slave carpenters. The Stagville Barn provides the most monumental evidence of the slave presence. Erected in 1860, when Paul Cameron owned Stagville, it demonstrates both the agricultural prosperity of the 1850s and the capabilities of the plantation craftsmen.

Stagville today is a seventy-one acre historic property owned by the state of North Carolina and is located in the northern section of Durham County. Since opening in 1977, Stagville Center has offered a wide array of seminars, workshops, and conferences on topics such as historic preservation, African-American studies, and garden history. Many of Stagville's programs have been sponsored jointly with area universities such as Duke and North Carolina Central, as well as with such organizations as Old Salem, Inc., and Colonial Williamsburg.

Historians, contractors, architects, homeowners, and many others from across the region and nation have journeyed to the Center to attend such programs. Their activities utilize Stagville's collection of historic structures together with a large, modern classroom building. Stagville Center operates under the authority of the Division of Archives and History of the North Carolina Department of Cultural Resources. The Stagville Center Corporation provides further support. Together with this nonprofit corporation, the Friends of Stagville and the Stagville Associates provide special funding and "hands-on" help with center programming. This information was gleaned from the brochure, "Stagville." Stagville Center is *open Monday-Friday, 9:00 a.m. to 4:00 p.m.* ADMISSION IS FREE. *Directions:*

Follow route 501 Business (Roxboro Road) north from Durham and turn right on State Road 1004 (Old Oxford Highway). Stagville Center is on S.R. 1004, seven miles from 501 Business. Look for Stagville's white hanging sign on the right.

Emmanuel A.M.E. Church

The Emmanuel A.M.E. Church erected in 1888 is the oldest surviving religious edifice built by a Durham congregation. The land and building materials for the church were donated by Richard Burton Fitzgerald, Durham's foremost Black businessman of the late nineteenth century. He and his family supported the church for more than eight decades. The significance of the Emmanuel A.M.E. Church is multi-faceted. The building is architecturally noteworthy, as a handsome example of the popular Gothic Revival style. As an

Emmanuel A.M.E. Church

early structure raised by a Black institution in a city which has experienced rapid growth and redevelopment almost continuously since it began in the 1850s, the Emmanuel A.M.E. Church has gained additional importance in recent decades. Since the late 1940s, all of Durham's other early Black churches have disappeared for a variety of reasons after their congregations erected replacement buildings, usually less distinctive than the originals. Furthermore, Emmanuel A.M.E. Church, serving as both a spiritual sanctuary and community center, represents the development of a Black community in the neighborhood of West End. It is the most distinguished of the few remaining buildings associated with one of Durham's most influential Black families, the Fitzgeralds. The building is presently used by the Deliverance Temple Holy Church and is located at **706 Kent Street.**

St. Joseph's A.M.E. Church

St. Joseph's A.M.E. Church, built in 1891 by Philadelphia architect, Samuel L. Leary, stands as one of Durham's more interesting vernacular examples of late Victorian religious architecture. In both plan and composition, it is a highly eclectic work, combining dense massing of Richardsonian Romanesque with elements derived from the Gothic Revival, as well as the Neo-Classical movement. The bricks for the church were fired in the brickyards of Robert B. Fitzgerald, a Black who came to Durham's Station from Pennsylvania in 1886, established his brickworks, and eventually became first president of the Mechanics and Farmers Bank when it was established in February 1907. Early on in the building of the church, Washington Duke and Julian S. Carr, tobacco capitalists, contributed heavily to the building fund. The memorial windows in the church sanctuary commemorate their generosity. St. Joseph's congregation eventually built a new church. The old building is presently used as a cultural center. It is located at **2521 Fayetteville Street.** Phone (919) 683-1379.

J. C. Scarborough House

The J. C. Scarborough House was built in 1916. Mr. Scarborough moved from Kinston to Durham in 1906 and opened Scarborough and Hargett Funeral Home, Durham's first funeral service for Blacks. Until his death in 1972 at the age of ninety-four, Scarborough remained active in his business, which continues today as Durham's preeminent Black funeral service, run by Scarborough's children and grandchildren. Scarborough was one of the foremost leaders of Durham's Black community, serving as a director of Mechanics and

J.C. Scarborough House

Farmers Bank, secretary of Lincoln Hospital, and a trustee of St. Joseph's A.M.E. Church. One of his greatest contributions was the establishment of the Daisy E. Scarborough Home (now Scarborough Nursery School) in the mid-1920s in memory of his first wife. The family has carefully preserved the Scarborough House, the most distinctive example of the surrounding neighborhood's prestige throughout the early decades of this century. Constructed largely with materials salvaged from one of Durham's finest Queen Anne houses, the Scarborough House is notable for its interior displaying the city's most extensive collection of "high style" architectural elements from the Victorian period.

This house is located at **1406 Fayetteville Street near North Carolina Central University.** *(PRIVATE RESIDENCE)*

Although the Scarborough House is the largest and most imposing home on Fayetteville Street and Southeast Durham, there are a number of other significant Black-owned houses. They all are *PRIVATE RESIDENCES.* They include:

The F. K. Watkins House. This two-story frame house was built in 1915 and is located at **1218 Fayetteville Street.**

Dr. Charles H. Shepard House. Built in the late 1920s, this two-story house with stepped and rounded parapets at the attic dormer is located at **1601 Fayetteville Street.**

The Charles Pratt House. One of the oldest buildings in Durham, the Charles Pratt House is associated with one of the first two Black land-owning families in the county. This two-story frame house was built early in this century and is located at **1614 Fayetteville Street.**

Dr. Joseph Napoleon Mills House. Built in the late teens of this century, this large two-story, double-pile house with rear wings is located at **1211 Fayetteville Street.**

The Harris-Ingram House. This cross-gable roofed bungalow with rows of short and tall cypress shake shingles was built in 1921 and is located at **1213 Fayetteville Street.**

The John Pearson House. Built in 1921, this one and one-half-story house with cedar shake shingles at the peak of the gabled dormer is located at **1215 Fayetteville Street.**

The Alphonso Elder House. Constructed in 1931, this one-story, Tudor Cottage-style house with its arched entrance and irregular roof-line is located at **406 Formosa Street.**

The Thomas Fitzgerald House. Black contractor, Thomas Fitzgerald, built this house in the 1910s. He was the son of one of Durham's foremost brickmasters, Richard Fitzgerald. This two-story, brick house has a wraparound, one-story porch and a raised basement. This house is located at **802 Kent Street.**

Other significant buildings in the area include:

Pages Grocery. This gable-front store with a shed-roofed porch dates from the late 1930s and is located at **1304 Fayetteville Street.**

Stanford L. Warren Public Library. Constructed in 1940, it grew out of a Sunday School library at White Rock Baptist Church which Dr. Aaron M. Moore began in 1913. Three years later, Dr. Moore, John Merrick, and others raised funds to build a new library on Fayetteville and East Pettigrew Streets. In 1940, Stanford L. Warren, president of the Library Board, donated the land for the site of the present building. Consequently, the library was named in his honor. This was a fitting honor for a man who had served as leader of the Library Board for more than fifteen years. This brick Colonial Revival-style building, with a large Palladian window in each end elevation, is

Stanford L. Warren Public Library

reported to house the second oldest Black library in North Carolina. The library is located at **1201 Fayetteville Street.**

Gesthemene Baptist Church. Erected in the early 1920s, this is thought to be the oldest wooden church in southeast Durham. Gesthemene Baptist Church is a gable-front building with a two-panel, Greek Revival door. The church with its lancet tinted windows is located at **100 West Enterprise Street.**

The Kyles Temple A.M.E. Zion Church. Many believe the distinguishing feature of this building, erected in 1930, is its front porch, recessed and surrounded by a wide arch which becomes almost a half-circle at the stairs. The church has a gable-front frame with a square tower at a front corner. It also has rectangular, stained-glass windows. The church is located at **409 Dunstan Street.**

Mechanics and Farmers Bank Building. This six-story structure was built in 1921 in Neo-Classical Revival style. Over the years, Mechanics and Farmers Bank has provided financial and moral support to Durham's Black community. It is located at **116 Parrish Street.**

HILLSBOROUGH

Dickerson Chapel

Dickerson Chapel of the A.M.E. Church was organized in the late nineteenth century by Reverends Job Berry and Billy Payne . It was remodeled in 1891, and again in 1947. It first served as the courthouse of Orange County. In 1845, Reverend Elias Dodson, a White Baptist preacher, bought the old courthouse and moved it to the corner of Churton and Queen Streets, converting it to the First Baptist Church of Hillsborough. In 1862, the Baptist Church sold the house and lot to George Bishop. Bishop sold it to Ellerton P. Morris, Anthony M. Krinton, and Richard Cadbaerry of Philadelphia for $1,200.00. These men were designated as "friends of the colored free man" of Hillsborough.

At first Quakers used the building as a school for Black children. Young women from Pennsylvania were sent to Hillsborough to educate the children. The school was sold to members of Dickerson Chapel in 1886. Job Berry was the first pastor of the chapel before and after the purchase. The original, massive hand-hewn beams of Hillsborough's third courthouse may still be seen in the church's basement. Copper sheathing was placed on the steeple in the mid-1960s. The church continues to offer spiritual and social support to the Black community of Hillsborough, as it has for over one hundred years. Some of this historical data was supplied by the church which is located **off of I-40, in downtown Hillsborough, at the junction of East Queen and Churton Streets on the southeast corner.**

RALEIGH

The Berry O'Kelly Memorial

Berry O'Kelly

The Berry O'Kelly Memorial was erected by sixty-five members of the Berry O'Kelly School's alumni and friends on December 22, 1985. The inscription on the memorial identifies O'Kelly as "Humanitarian, Leader in Business and Education." Berry O'Kelly was born in Wake County ca. 1864. He served as chairman of the local school committee and in 1914, succeeded in consolidating three rural Black schools in Wake County into the Berry O'Kelly Training School, a four-year high school, in the section of Raleigh known as Method. He served as chairman of the school committee while H. L. Trigg was its principal. It had eight teachers and was one of only three schools to be accredited by the state of North Carolina. The students were required to complete fifteen units before they could graduate, including science, mathematics, history, and language. The students were also taught vocational agriculture, food, clothing, and economics. The school was later used as an elementary school and closed in 1966 after serving the Black community for over fifty years. During the tenure of the school, hundreds of students graduated from it and went on to become productive citizens of the nation.

Besides being an educator, Berry O'Kelly was also a successful businessman. He owned a general store, realty company, and shoe company. He was also chairman of a life insurance company and vice-president of the Raleigh branch of the Mechanics and Farmers Bank of Durham. The memorial is located at **500 Method Road between Method Park and St. James A.M.E. Church.**

Saint Augustine's College

Saint Augustine's College was founded in 1867 by the Episcopal Church as a college for Blacks, and has been designated as an historic district. The college is located **on Edenton Street.** St. Augustine's College Historic District includes the following buildings:

St. Agnes Hospital dates from 1909 and is a three-story, stone cruciform structure which served as a hospital from its construction until 1961. It is now partially in use for college administrative functions. The hospital was designed by Paul A. Davis of Philadelphia.

Goold Hall, a modified, H-shaped structure of brick, was built in 1930 as a nurses' home for the hospital. It was expanded and converted to a women's dormitory in 1961.

Tuttle Building, erected in 1925, is a rectangular brick building constructed to house the Bishop Tuttle School of Social and Church Work. It came into the possession of the college after the Tuttle School closed in 1941 for World War II and subsequently failed to reopen. It now houses ROTC.

The Cheshire Building, a two-story, rectangular brick structure with Classical Revival detailing, was built in 1930 as a dining hall and domestic science classroom facility. It now houses college offices.

Delaney Hall was built in 1930. It is a rectangular brick building with Classical Revival detailing. It has always served as a women's dormitory.

Penick Hall of Science is a rectangular, brick building built in 1950 for the science departments and is still in use as such.

The Art Building is a square, two-story brick structure built in 1919 as a model school for the normal course. It has since also served as the science building.

The Hunter Building is an H-shaped, brick building with Classical Revival detailing, built in 1924 to partially replace the Lyman Building in providing administrative and classroom space. It now houses only offices.

The Benson Library is a cruciform stone structure, constructed in 1930. It served as a library until 1972 and now houses college offices.

Taylor Hall was built in two parts. The first Benson Library is its east end, built in 1898 as an L-shaped stone structure. In 1902, the rectangular stone structure on the west end was added and named Taylor Hall. The name came to indicate the whole building after the construction of the second Benson Library. It is used for miscellaneous purposes at present.

The Chapel was built in 1895. It began as a rectangular stone structure with a tower, and was modified with a north transept in 1904 and south transept in 1917 which replaced the tower. A lych gate was added in 1903. The Chapel remains in use.

The Infirmary Building, constructed in 1914 to house the trades departments, is a brick two-story structure. The building served as infirmary for many years and now serves as a laundry and women's dormitory space.

Masonic Temple

The Masonic Temple building, constructed in 1907, housed the Widow's Son Lodge No. 4, established in 1867 by Bishop James W. Hood, a prominent Black missionary and social leader in Raleigh. The temple also housed the Excelsior Lodge No. 21, established in 1879. Several prominent, post-Civil War Black leaders, such as publisher James H. Young and North Carolina state representative Stewart Ellison, were associated with these benevolent fraternal associations. By locating the building in southeast Raleigh, the Masons helped to draw other Black institutions, businesses, and residents into the neighborhood. This contributed to the creation of a close-knit, vital Black society there. The building itself is a simple three-story, brick box with Italianate details. There is commercial space on the first floor, office space on the second floor, and an assembly hall on the third. The structure has provided the physical expression of the idea of a united Black community throughout its history. It is well recognized for the role it has played in the betterment of Black economic and social life in the capital. The building is located at **427 South Blount Street.**

St. Paul's Church

The congregation which formed St. Paul's Church in 1865 was the slave membership of the Edenton Street Methodist Church. The Black members attended services there until 1846, but due to the rapid growth of the congregation, it became necessary for the Blacks to attend their own services in the church basement. This arrangement continued until 1853 when the White Methodists bought old Christ Church, a wooden building located on the corner of New Bern Avenue and Wilmington Street. The Black membership moved the old church to the corner of Edenton and Harrington Streets where they began to hold their services in 1854, according to Alice Carrington Jones. The Black congregation remained under the guidance of the Methodist Episcopal Church South until Emancipation. In 1865, the membership severed its ties with the Methodist Episcopal Church and joined the African Methodist Episcopal Conference, a Black denomination organized by Richard Allen in 1816. At the South Carolina Conference of the A.M.E. Church, Bishop Daniel A. Payne appointed the Reverend George A. Broadie from the Canada Conference as the pastor of St. Paul's Church in Raleigh, thereby giving the church its first Black pastor and establishing the denomination in the city.

The ministers of St. Paul's Church took a leading role in the organization of Black political activity during the Reconstruction Era. Blacks in North Carolina held their first lawful assembly at St. Paul's Church in 1865. Delegates from a two hundred mile radius gathered at the church and drafted a series of proposals calling for the repeal of unjust racial laws and for the betterment of the social condition of the Black race in North Carolina. Throughout the post-bellum period, the pastors and the membership of St. Paul's Church continued the spirit of that first lawful meeting of Blacks, providing the state with some of its finest Black spokesmen in the Reverend Henry Eppes, Stewart Ellison, and the Reverend R.W.H. Leak. The church

was destroyed by a fire in 1909. It was rebuilt in June 1910. Today,
this edifice still houses the St. Paul's A.M.E. congregation which has
worshipped on this lot as both slaves and free men for almost 140
years. It is an inspirational symbol of the hardships and sacrifices of
its congregation. This Gothic-style church is located at **402 West
Edenton Street.**

St. Paul's Church

Shaw University

In 1873, according to the school records, "Estey Seminary," as it
was first called, was erected to serve women students. Jacob Estey of
Brattleboro, Vermont, and George Morse of Putname, Connecticut,
were substantial contributors toward the construction of the building.

The 1874-1875 catalogue of the school described Estey Hall in glowing terms:

> Estey Hall: This is the finest school building in the state, and is the pride of the colored people of North Carolina, as it affords facilities for the education of their daughters. It will accommodate about one hundred pupils, and the large number of young ladies from the best families in the state, during the first session, has proved (sic) the necessity and wisdom of this undertaking. The school is destined to be a Fountain of Light, and it is earnestly hoped that some lover of female education will amply endow this department of the school.

Estey Hall is a major landmark of south Raleigh, a handsome and imposing Victorian institutional building whose bold ornamentation complements its large scale. As the oldest surviving building of Shaw University, it is one of the important monuments of North Carolina's Black history and is prominent in the history of the education of Black women. The building is located on **South Street.**

St. James A.M.E. Church

St. James A.M.E. Church was founded in 1923 by a group of Blacks who saw the need to build a church in the western part of Raleigh. One of the leaders of the church was Berry O'Kelly, educator, businessman, and leader. The church is built in the Gothic Revival style and is a good example of this style in ecclesiastical architecture. It has arched, stained-glass windows.

St. James A.M.E. Church and its congregation have been a positive force in the western section of Raleigh and have contributed greatly to both the spiritual and secular well-being of the city and state. The church is located at **520 Method Road.**

St. James A.M.E. Church

TRIAD REGION

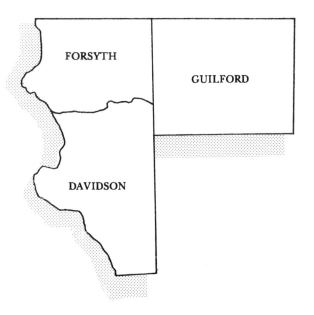

Greensboro
High Point
Sedalia
Thomasville
Winston-Salem

GREENSBORO

North Carolina A&T State University

North Carolina A&T State University, founded in 1899, has graduated many prominent national figures, including Reverend Jesse Jackson and astronaut Ron McNair. A number of buildings on its campus are listed on the National Register of Historic Places. They include:

Noble Hall. This building was constructed in 1922 and named to honor Marcus C. S. Noble, long-time chairman of the University's Board of Trustees. This three-story building has a full basement, nine bays wide and three bays deep, and contains 20,672 square feet of office and classroom space. Rusticated brick quoins define the corners of the rectangular building, and the first story brickwork simulates smooth rustication.

Dudley Memorial Building. The centerpiece of the campus and its most architecturally distinctive building, Dudley Memorial was designed by prominent Greensboro architect, Charles C. Hartmann, and constructed in 1930. It is located on the site of the university's first administration building which had burned earlier that year. Both buildings were named Dudley Memorial to honor the university's second president, James Benson Dudley (1896-1925). It features the most lavish application of stone of any of the campus buildings. Stone is used for quoins, a string course, a broad steep of fifteen steps to the main entrance, smooth-faced blocks defining a five bay entrance, intricately carved lintels, acroteria, full classical entablature, and splayed arches with keystones over the eight-over-twelve, sash windows. There is also an elegant and imposing hexastyle, Ionic portico with an incised frieze. The building is unaltered except for the double-leaf, metal-trimmed, plate glass entrance doors, which replace the original doors.

The Dudley Memorial Building

Morrison Hall. Constructed in 1924 and named for North Carolina governor Cameron Morrison (1921-1925), this dormitory building is almost identical to Noble Hall, except that it is eleven bays wide, and that rusticated stone, rather than brick, surrounds the main entrance. Also, the incised stone name panel above the nonfunctional balcony extends to surround the center third-story windows as well. Morrison Hall retains the original double-leaf, main entrance doors.

Murphy Hall. This one-story, 26,002 square-foot building is thirteen bays wide and three bays deep. It was constructed in 1923 and used for many years as the student cafeteria. The symmetrical structure is distinguished by a projecting pedimental, three bay entrance pavilion with rusticated brick and a full-height, arched, rusticated brick door. The pavilion is also ornamented with four full-height brick pilasters with stone capitals and bases, stone panels carved in an urn and garland motif, and a full entablature in the pediment. The building was remodeled in 1977.

Richard B. Harrison Auditorium. This rectangular, flat-roofed, two-story building with a full basement at the rear was constructed in 1939 by the Federal Works Agency of the Public Works Administration for use as the university's main auditorium. According to a lobby plaque, Leon McMinn was the architect and H. L. Coble, the contractor. Ornamentation on this austere building is confined to the seven bay main entrance with the bays defined by plain brick pilasters, simply molded stone bases, and capitals. The auditorium seats approximately one thousand (twenty-five rows on the ground floor and ten rows in the shallow balcony). The auditorium is named for Richard Berry Harrison who taught drama and directed plays at the A&T State University.

Besides having a number of very fine historical buildings on campus, A&T has the **Mattye Reed African Heritage Museum**. The African Heritage Center includes a growing collection which has now reached over six thousand items from some thirty-five African countries, the United States, and several other areas. Many of the items on display, such as pots, baskets, dishes, jewelry, weapons, and fabrics, are of a functional nature, reflecting traditional and contemporary life of various ethnic cultures. Prominent parts of the museum collection are masks, icons, and sculptures in bronze, ivory, and wood which reflect the regional and cultural traditions of the people who produced them. Some furniture made by Thomas Day is also on display.

Throughout the year, the center has on exhibit its permanent collection as well as a number of special exhibits of sculpture, paintings, graphics, and other media. The complex is already used as a resource center for students, teachers, and researchers from nursery, primary, secondary education, and institutions of higher education in the Piedmont region. It is anticipated that the center will serve also as focal point for cooperative activity between several departments of the university and neighboring institutions of higher education. This activity will consist of ethnic heritage studies and programs, a series of educational TV programs, and preparations of slides and film strips for use in schools of North Carolina and other parts of the United States. The information for the African Heritage Museum was supplied by the Museum. It is located on A&T State University campus at **200 Nocho Street.** *It is opened by appointment.* Phone (919) 379-7374.

There is a bust of Ronald McNair in front of the R.E. McNair Hall of the School of Engineering. McNair was born in 1950 and was a graduate of A&T State University. He became an astronaut and was killed along with six others on the space shuttle Challenger, January 28, 1986.

Bennett College

Although Bennett College was founded in 1873, it does not have any of its original buildings. Its three oldest buildings presently in use were erected in 1922. There is also the Carnegie Building which was built around 1918. It was originally constructed as a library and is now used for storage. The other buildings are as follows:

Robert E. Jones Hall was erected in 1922. This three-story, Corinthian-style building was named for Bishop Robert Elijah Jones (1872-1960), first Black bishop of the Methodist Episcopal Church.

John H. Race Administration Building was erected in 1922. In 1925, this two-story building with its ornamental masonry and Italianate style of architecture was named for Dr. John H. Race, a trustee and benefactor of the college.

Wilbur F. Steele Hall was also erected in 1922. This one-story, rectangular structure with its ornamental masonry and Ionic columns was named for Wilbur F. Steele, president of Bennett College from 1881-1889.

HIGH POINT

William Penn High School/High Point Normal and Industrial Institute

The William Penn High School/High Point Normal and Industrial Institute grounds contain three buildings, dating from ca. 1910 to 1930. These are major community landmarks significant in High Point's Black history. The Institute, founded by Quaker philanthropists, was moved from Asheboro, North Carolina to High Point in 1891, where it served the Black community of the region for thirty-three years. After 1924, when the school became part of the city's public school system, the name was changed to William Penn reflecting the importance of the Quakers throughout its early history. As William Penn High School, it continued as an all-Black school until 1968 when it was closed. Many of the city's community, business, and intellectual leaders either taught or were educated here. Two of the buildings are industrial-type structures erected to house the activities related to a manual training curriculum which was offered in addition to academic training. A large Colonial Revival structure, remodelled and enlarged to its present appearance in 1930, is the campus' focal point. The school building is located on **Washington Drive between Eccles Place and Gaylord Court.**

High Point Normal Institute

The Kilby Hotel

The Kilby Hotel is a handsome brick structure located on Washington Avenue in High Point. The building, with its fine brick-work and interior features, typical of early twentieth century hotels, is a good example of commercial structures of this period and a rare survivor in a city which has lost much of its early commercial architecture. Built ca. 1910 by Mrs. Nannie Kilby, a prominent Black businesswoman, the building is now owned by the third generation of that family who continue to operate and maintain the hotel. The hotel is located at **627 East Washington Street.** Phone (919) 884-9830.

The Kilby Hotel

SEDALIA

Palmer Memorial Institute

Charlotte Eugenia Hawkins Brown was born on June 11, 1883, in Henderson, North Carolina. During her childhood, her family moved to Cambridge, Massachusetts, where she attended the Cambridge English and Latin School. She later attended the State Normal School of Salem, Massachusetts. While a student there, Miss

Part of the Palmer Memorial Institute complex

Hawkins was offered a teaching position in North Carolina by the American Missionary Association.

Before accepting the position, Charlotte was assured by her principal at the State Normal School that she would be allowed to complete her own school work in the summer months in order to graduate. The eighteen year old Charlotte Hawkins returned to North Carolina in 1901 to teach rural Black children in a church/schoolhouse in what is now known as Sedalia, located about ten miles east of Greensboro. The school closed just one year after her arrival. But, appeasing the wishes of local community residents, Charlotte decided to remain and establish her own school. She spent a year raising the money in New England before she founded the Alice Freeman Palmer Memorial Institute, a day and boarding school for Blacks. The school was named in honor of a New England educator who had given Charlotte Hawkins both financial support and help in fundraising for the project. Alice Freeman Palmer was also the first woman president of Wellesley College located in Massachusetts.

Under the leadership of Dr. Charlotte Hawkins Brown, Palmer Memorial Institute acquired 350 acres, several buildings, and a solid reputation for education. The school included a sizeable farm on which the students grew much of their own food. The students in the industrial department helped to build several of the present buildings on campus.

Dr. Brown worked tirelessly to make Palmer Institute a place of educational excellence. She oversaw the growth of Palmer's physical plant and, most importantly, guided the lives of her students. Palmer

Early faculty of the Palmer Memorial Institute. Charlotte Hawkins Brown is center, back row.

grew to become one of the nation's leading preparatory schools for Blacks. Brown was president of Palmer Memorial Institute for fifty years. During that time, she served in many public and community positions: The Young Women's Christian Association (YWCA), North Carolina Teachers Association, State Council of Defense, Alpha

Kappa Alpha Sorority, National Association of Colored Women, North Carolina Federation of Women's Clubs, the Urban League, and Federal Council of Churches. She also received several honorary degrees from institutions such as Wilberforce and Lincoln Universities. Besides being an educator, she was also an author. She wrote *The Correct Thing to Do, to Say, to Wear* (1941) and *Mammy: An Appeal to the Heart of the South* (1919).

During Dr. Brown's tenure as president of Palmer Memorial, over one thousand students graduated. Most went on to become productive citizens for the state and nation. Dr. Brown died January 11, 1961. In 1971, Palmer Memorial Institute closed its doors. The school is now a state historic site, the first to honor a Black individual, and was opened to the public in November 1987. It features programs such as exhibits, tours of historic structures, a bookstore, and audiovisual presentations. The center is planning a Black history resource center, which will include a library with computer facilities. It is open *April 1 through October 31, Monday-Saturday, 9:00 to 5:00, and Sunday, 1:00 to 5:00; November 1 through March 31, Tuesday-Saturday, 10:00 to 4:00, Sunday, 1:00 to 4:00. Closed Monday.* ADMISSION IS FREE.

THOMASVILLE

Church Street School

The Church Street School was built as a part of a project that also included companion White schools in Thomasville (Kern Street School) and nearby Lexington (Grimes School). It was constructed between 1935 and 1937 under a combination of a PWA grant and local money and was the first brick school facility in Thomasville for Black people. It was originally a consolidated school that included all grades and represented a considerable commitment by the community for the education of its Black youth, who attended there until 1968 when the school system was integrated. Church Street School was built as an up-to-date school facility according to the standards of the time, and was designed by a well-known Winston-Salem architect, William Roy Wallace (1890-1983). The Church Street and Kern Street Schools are the only known surviving buildings by Wallace in Thomasville. Church Street School was an important institution in the Black community in Thomasville for more than thirty years. This building desperately needs repairs and should be preserved. The school building is located at **27 Church and Jasper Streets.**

WINSTON-SALEM

The Atkins House

The Atkins House was built by Simon Green Atkins in 1893 and was the first house to be constructed in the Columbian Heights neighborhood of Winston-Salem. Dr. Atkins was the most prominent resident of the Columbian Heights area, due to his efforts in establishing this new neighborhood and the founding of Slater Industrial Academy. Atkins' additional community activities included his involvement in the opening of the Columbian Heights High School and the founding of the Slater School Hospital, the first for Blacks in Winston-Salem. Slater Industrial Academy, later Winston-Salem State University, was Atkins' greatest achievement. He served as president of the academy from 1892 until shortly before his death on June 28, 1934. Although the Atkins House has had extensive remodelling over the years, including new siding, it is significant because its form and simplicity are typical of thousands which were built in the state in the late nineteenth century, but many of which were torn down. The Atkins House is located across the street from Winston-Salem State University at **346 Atkins Street.**

The Atkins House

The Winston-Salem Delta Fine Arts

The Winston-Salem Delta Fine Arts was incorporated in 1972 by the Winston-Salem Alumnae Chapter of Delta Sigma Theta Sorority, Inc., as a nonprofit subsidiary. Its mission is:

- To stimulate community interest in American arts and humanities, with emphasis on Afro-Americans' contributions to the arts and humanities in America;

- To foster increased awareness and knowledge of Afro-Americans' contributions to the arts and humanities in America;
- To encourage individual creativity;
- To build pride in Afro-Americans' contributions to arts and humanities in America.

Today, Delta Fine Arts is Winston-Salem's oldest incorporated Afro-American nonprofit cultural organization. Most of its activities are held in the Delta Arts Center, established by Delta Fine Arts in

The Delta Fine Arts Center

1982. The Center is the city's only one of its kind operated by a community-based, Black public service organization. Some of its activities include arts and humanities classes, lectures, workshops, exhibitions, and performances by professional artists. Many of their programs are conducted by resident artists representing visual arts, music, drama, and crafts. Delta Fine Arts' exhibition programs include both locally curated and national traveling shows such as those circulated by the Smithsonian Institution. Much of this information was taken from the "Delta Arts Center Brochure." The center is located **near I-40 at 1511 East Third Street.** It is *open 10:00 a.m.-5:30 p.m. Monday-Friday. Call for weekend hours.* Phone (919) 722-2625. ADMISSION IS FREE.

Winston-Salem State University

Winston-Salem State University, formerly Slater Industrial Academy, unfortunately does not have any of its original buildings. It does, however, have a number of buildings which were constructed between 1918-1925. They are as follows:

The Alumni and Public Relations Building was constructed in 1918 and is the oldest building on campus. It was originally built as the Home Economics and Practical Arts Building. The name was changed in 1945, when it was renovated. This two-story building has a Corinthian Revival-style entrance, with two columns, which stands out from the rest of this Art Deco-style building.

Bickett Hall was erected in 1921 and originally used as a women's dormitory. It was named in honor of Thomas W. Bickett, who served as governor of North Carolina between 1917 and 1921. This building has six tall columns across its main entrance and is built in the Romanesque Revival style. Bickett Hall is presently used as a men's dormitory.

Colson Hall was constructed in 1921 as a dormitory for freshmen women and was used as an annex to Atkins Hall with a connecting link which was sealed off in 1945. This square building is four stories high with two columns on the front entrance. It was named for Mrs. Kate D. Colson, the first matron of Atkins. She was also at one time the Dean of Women.

President House was built in 1924 and housed each president until 1980 when the president's residence was moved off campus. This two-story home has a wide porch with Corinthian-like columns, hipped roof, and two dormer windows, giving the appearance of an attic. Two chimneys, one on each side of the house, grace this structure.

Carolina Hall was built in 1925 as a classroom building. For many years it was the largest classroom structure on campus. This rectangular two-story building, named after the state, has a Corinthian column entrance.

Besides the above buildings on campus, the university has **Two Stone Arches** that were built by Black stone mason, James Higgins. The graduating class of 1936 commissioned Mr. Higgins to make the arches. A marker on one arch states, "To the Memory of Dr. Simon Green Atkins (1863-1934), Educator, Benefactor, Founder and Builder of the Winston-Salem Teachers College, Class of 1936." The marker on the other arch reads, "Oleona Pegram Atkins, in recognition of her unselfish service and loyal devotion to Winston-Salem Teachers College, Class of 1936." The arches are located between the Hauser Student Union and Carolina Hall buildings.

Winston-Salem State University also has a Sculpture Garden that includes the following pieces:

"Southern Sunrise" by Mel Edwards is a twelve-foot-high stainless steel piece, geometric in shape. Its surface is polished and painted with various sized shapes. It was erected on the campus in 1983.

"Arbor Spirit" by Roberto Bertoia is a four-foot-high wooden sculpture. He carved this massive, yet graceful, work in his studio in Ithaca, New York, and transported it by truck to Winston-Salem, where it was erected in 1985.

"Po Tolo" is a massive sculpture of stone and steel, eight feet high and forty feet in diameter, by Tyrone Mitchell. The name, "Po Tolo," is Dogon for the star Sirius. The Dogon people live in Mali, West Africa. This piece was designed for the space created by the converging wings of the RJR Business School Building. This work was placed on campus in 1985.

"Garden Ruins" consists of three 6,000 pound boulders and was designed by Beverly Buchanan, a painter and sculptor. The three rocks are three, five, and six feet high and were placed on campus in 1984.

"Homage," a small colorful steel sculpture, was created by James Marlow. Ira and Ruth Julian, both Winston-Salem residents, donated this work to the university in 1975. It is now part of the outdoor garden.

Each of the above pieces of sculpture, except the latter one, was commissioned by the university. All the pieces are contemporary works, and university officials contend that these works comprise the only outdoor public sculpture garden in North Carolina.

Another point of interest on campus is the **Diggs Gallery** which is located in the basement of the new library. This gallery, nearly seven thousand square feet in size, was named in honor of James "T." Diggs, Jr., who taught at the university for over forty years, also serving as chairman of the Art Department before he retired in 1979. Diggs died in April 1989. This gallery has a number of pieces of art on loan from Diggs' collection, as well as from those of Gordon Hanes, Glenda Wharton-Little, and others. It also has various exhibits from the Smithsonian Institution, the Winston-Salem Delta Fine Arts, Inc., the African Heritage Center at North Carolina A&T State University, the North Carolina Museum of Art, and from other institutions. The gallery is *open 11:00 a.m.-5:00 p.m., Tuesday through Friday and 2:00-5:00 p.m. on Sunday.*

Besides the Diggs Gallery, there is a two-panel mural in the atrium of new O'Kelly Library. The mural was painted by noted artist John Biggers and is entitled "Ascension" and "Origins."

The Society for the Study of Afro-American History

The Society for the Study of Afro-American History in Winston-Salem/Forsyth County, Inc., is the only Black historical society in Forsyth County. It is presently housed on the Winston-Salem State University campus. This nonprofit organization has the most complete materials on Black history and culture in Forsyth County. The society has hundreds of photographs, newspapers, tapes, videos, art works, and artifacts of significance to the county, state, and nation. The society produces exhibitions, an annual historical calendar and banquets. The office of the society is located in the old Nursing School Building at Winston-Salem State University. WSSU is located **off of I-40 and Martin Luther King, Jr. Drive.** *Call for appointment before you visit.* Phone (919) 750-2610.

St. Phillips Moravian Church

St. Phillips Moravian Church was established in 1822 in Salem, thus becoming the first Black church in Forsyth County and probably the first Black church in North Carolina. According to one report, the first meeting was held on March 24, 1822, at the home of Budney and Phoebe "in the Negro quarter of Salem Plantation." From 1822 until about 1869, the church was located on Church Street in Salem and had seventy-five to eighty members. In 1861, a new church was built adjacent to the old one which had burned down. The congregation enlarged the structure in 1890. This church was used until 1952 when it moved to a new location. This unique, Greek Revival-style church, with its rectangular structure and elaborate sawnwork balcony railing featuring a fleur-de-lis design, has housed an historically significant congregation. The church is located in **Old Salem at South Church Street and Race Street.**

Kyles Heights

The Kyles Home, now Kyles Heights, was built in the 1920s or 1930s for Lynwood Westinghouse Kyles. He was a bishop in the African Methodist Episcopal Zion Church. He graduated from Lincoln University in Pennsylvania, and is credited with building the largest and most efficient parsonage owned by Blacks in the United States at the time. Kyles Heights is a brick mansion with a tiled roof. This two-story house, with rooms protruding over the roof, has a wide wraparound porch and four chimneys. Bishop Kyles died July 8, 1941, and his last rites were held at Goler Memorial A.M.E. Zion Church in Winston-Salem. He is buried in that city. Kyles Heights is located at **1621 14th Street.**

Former home of Bishop Lynwood Kyles

NORTHERN
PIEDMONT
REGION

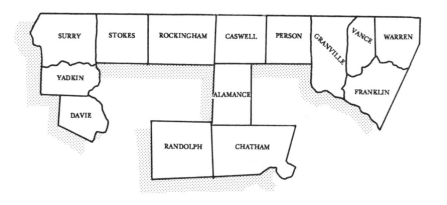

Eden	Oaks
Franklinton	Pine Hall
Madison	Reidsville
McCray	Shiloh
Milton	Warrenton

EDEN

Mt. Sinai Baptist Church

Mt. Sinai Baptist Church is located in the Rockingham County town of Eden (formerly Leaksville, Spray, and Draper) on the edge of a small Black neighborhood in old Leaksville. Mt. Sinai, formed in 1888, is the oldest Black Baptist church, as well as one of the two earliest separate churches for Blacks in this town. This striking sanctuary, built in 1921, is the second building of the congregation and one of the major Black landmarks in Eden. The earlier, small

Mt. Sinai Baptist Church

wooden church, no longer standing, was built ca. 1891 on a nearby site. Mt. Sinai was designed and built by the J. M. Hopper Construction Company. J. M. Hopper, who owned a large brick and lumberyard in town, was the area's pioneer builder from the late 1880s to the 1940s. The brick structure is a representative example of early twentieth century Gothic Revival ecclesiastical architecture, symbolic of urban sophistication during this period. In her 1986 Eden inventory publication, *A Tale of Three Cities,* architectural historian Claudia Roberts Brown wrote that Mt. Sinai "is the most architecturally distinctive of Eden's churches built by Black congregations." The church is located at **512 North Henry Street.**

FRANKLINTON

Albion Academy

The Albion Academy was founded in Franklinton by the Presbyterian Board of Missions for Blacks in 1878. This school was both an elementary and high school. Moses Aaron Hopkins was principal until 1885, when he was succeeded by John A. Savage. Dr. Savage was born in Louisburg, North Carolina, and received his college degree from Lincoln University. He was the main force of the Albion Academy. It was through his efforts that the school grew to be such a large and well-equipped facility. Dr. Savage's motto to his students was, "Make money, save money, and behave yourselves." When the State Department of Education began to accredit schools in the 1920s, the Albion Academy High School received an "A" rating. Dr. Savage died in 1933. His house is one of only two remaining buildings that mark the existence of Albion Academy. The structure was originally built ca. 1880 as a classroom and/or dormitory. Dr. Savage enlarged it ca. 1895 for use as his private residence. The house is currently rented as a duplex, while the former dining hall/laundry is owned and used by the Holiness Trinity Church. The house is located at **124 College Street, Franklinton.** *(PRIVATE RESIDENCES)*

MADISON

Madison Colored School

Madison Colored School was built in 1924, with a section added in 1938. It was used until 1950. After 1950, it was vacant for a number of years, after which it was used for storage purposes by a private company until the early 1980s. The 1938 building was subsequently renovated beginning in 1986 by a number of concerned Black residents, who completed these renovations in 1989. This structure has two long buildings with a double-door entrance connecting them. The school is presently used as a community center. Although the original building is unrecognizable because of the extensive renovations, the school is significant because it graduated hundreds of students who went on to become educated and productive citizens. Moreover, the building is important because it has a Black History Room, and this is the only place in the area that is collecting and preserving Black local history. This building is located on **West Decatur and McGeehee Streets.** *Open by appointment.*

McCRAY

McCray School

McCray School derives its name from the McCray Post Office in the northern Alamance County farm community. Albert Graham (1830-1916), a prominent Alamance County landowner, agreed to sell some land to the "colored people" for a school in 1915, but the deed for the McCray School was not recorded. Andrew Nash, a local carpenter, along with other McCray residents, built the small one-room structure between 1915 and 1916. A school for White students had been established in 1901 near the McCray Baptist Church, approximately two miles from the future McCray School for Blacks. Prior to the completion of their school, Black children attended the Arches Grove School, according to the Board of Education records.

McCray School is a simple, almost austere building. Modern plumbing was never installed and drinking water was obtained from

The McCray School Building

a nearby farm. A centrally located, wood-burning stove was the only source of heat. Parents chopped a supply of wood at the beginning of each school term, which ran from October to April. While the majority of rural schools featured rustic, homemade benches, the Alamance County Board of Education furnished the McCray School with long, factory-made benches with three small attached desks. Little is known about the background of the teachers who taught at the McCray School or their exact periods of employment. Ailene Ducks was the first teacher at the school. Other teachers included Mr.

Boydken, Louise R. Fox (1925-1929), Eunice Parker (resigned 1942), and Merle Brown McCrae who taught from 1929 until the school closed in 1951.

The declining enrollment at McCray and three other Alamance County Black schools prompted the School Board officials to develop a permanent consolidation plan. The Board approved the construction of a modern fourteen-room facility in 1949. This school was an addition to the Pleasant Grove Elementary and High School built in 1928, and was located approximately five miles from the McCray School. After serving the community for thirty-five years, McCray School closed when the new consolidated school opened on September 14, 1951. Over the years, the school provided the Black residents in this community with a strong focal point, and parents were actively involved in school activities such as recitals, plays, and fund-raisers. The one-room McCray School is the only one remaining of its kind in Alamance County. This is certainly one of the best-preserved, one-room schools for Blacks in North Carolina, and more preservation is now underway. The school house is located on **the northwest side of N. NC 62 near McCray Primitive Baptist Church in McCray.**

MILTON

Union Tavern

Thomas Day, a free Black man, purchased Union Tavern in 1848. It was reported at one time to have been the largest and finest tavern in the area, but Day did not run it as such. Local records state he converted it into a residence and workshop. Day was a cabinet and furniture maker. He made fine bedsteads, chairs, tables, French sofas, benches, pews, etc. At one time, he employed about twelve Black and White workers in his shop. Thomas Day lived in the old

Union Tavern until 1858. This two-story, gabled brick building was six bays wide and two bays deep, with a one-story, wooden wing at the southeast (rear) corner, a wooden porch on the east side, and a brick and wooden wing on the west side. The brick facade was laid in Flemish bond, and that of the remaining three sides was laid in one-to-three common bond.

Day died in 1861. Over the years, the tavern has undergone several structural changes, and part of it was recently destroyed by fire. It is located on **NC 62/57 (southside of Broad Street at the southeast corner of Farmer's Alley).**

Woodside Inn

Woodside Inn was originally a large plantation house, built in the 1800s and later renovated. It is now a Bed and Breakfast Inn. Much of its woodwork was done by Thomas Day. It is open for tourists and private parties daily. Dinner is offered Thursday, Friday, and Saturday, and Brunch is served on Sunday. The Woodside Inn is located **about five miles from Milton.** Phone (919) 234-8646.

OAKS

Cooper School

The Cooper School is one of two remaining early twentieth century schoolhouses built for Black students in rural Alamance County. It is the only surviving structure of a small educational complex which was located on the grounds of the first Mary's Grove Congregational Church. The church was established in 1883 by the American Missionary Association in the Oaks community. Constructed ca. 1900, the Cooper School was used as a parsonage for the ministers of Mary's Grove until the early 1930s. Unlike the public McCray School in Alamance County, Cooper School was privately funded by the American Missionary Association. The one-room, wooden school-house has a gable-front roof, a plain exterior, and twin entrances for male and female students. It is located **behind Mary's Grove Congregational Church on SR 2143, Mary's Grove Church Road, in Oaks.**

The Cooper School

PINE HALL

Pine Hall Colored School

The Pine Hall Colored School started as a public school for White children around 1885. There was a one-teacher school on Hickory Fork Road about one and a quarter miles northwest of the present village of Pine Hall. Some years later, as the building deteriorated, the school was moved to the plantation of J. E. Dalton who had donated land for that purpose. It was agreed in 1905 to give the Dalton School to Blacks, who attended there until about 1910. Later the building was moved to Pole Bridge, and school was held there for some years.

Between 1914 and 1915, the Blacks again moved it to about a mile northeast of where it is presently located. On October 7, 1915, W. M. Chilsom deeded the present site to the County Board of Education, which consisted of S. P. Christian, Wilson Mitchell, and M. A. Martin. In 1916, Hedge Gibson moved a room there and placed it to the right of the school.

Up to 1942, the following teachers had taught at the school:

Plummer Hairston	Gertrude Carter
Pearl Carter	Ada Beesloe
Cora Hairston	Annie E. Hairston
Tula Goolsby	Olivia M. Leake
Lula Turner	Mary Carter
W. G. Hairston	

The superintendents were J. T. Smith and J. C. Carson, Sr.

The one-room schoolhouse served the Black children of the Pine Hall Community from the 1940s until 1952, when this and all the other Stokes County Black elementary schools were consolidated with the newly built London School in Walnut Cove. When this occurred, the Pine Hall Baptist Church purchased the old school building, along with approximately one acre of land. The school building is now just across the road from the church, and has been maintained in a limited way by the Pine Hall Baptist Church congregation since 1952. The members of the church and other Black citizens in the Pine Hall area, including those who have attended the school, have a sense of pride in the schoolhouse. Even though what it had to offer in the way of educational facilities and equipment was extremely limited, it nevertheless provided them with their first formal education. The schoolhouse is located on **Pole Bridge Road.**

REIDSVILLE

First Baptist Church

The building which was the home of the Black First Baptist Church in Reidsville from its construction in 1918 until the mid-1970s is a representative example of early twentieth century Gothic Revival ecclesiastical architecture in a small town setting. Organized in 1874 by Black members of the Reidsville Baptist Church, First Baptist was the first separate church for Blacks in the town, part of a larger movement to organize such churches during Reconstruction and the post-Reconstruction era. It has remained the leading Black Baptist congregation in Reidsville up to the present day. The relatively intact building stands on the edge of Reidsville's central business district in an area which, for much of the twentieth century, was a Black residential area. It replaced an earlier wooden structure built between 1883 and 1890 on an adjacent lot to the east. It was, in turn, replaced by a new facility in 1975. The attractive brick building has a typical gabled facade flanked by multi-stage towers of unequal heights, with a three-part tracery, stained-glass window centered on the facade; stained-glass windows in the bays of the side elevation; and a rose window on the rear elevation. The building is presently used by the Deliverance Temple Cathedral. The church is located at **401 South Scales Street (southwest corner of South Scales and** Williams Streets).

Former First Baptist Church, Reidsville

SHILOH

Gwynn Colored School

Gwynn Colored School is a one-room country school built by Robert Gwynn, a Black man, in 1879. Gwynn was born around 1814 and died between 1900 and 1910. There is no record of his early schooling; therefore, it is likely that he was self-educated. According to Joann Marie Davis, a descendant of Mr. Gwynn, he was a certified third-grade teacher as well as a large landowner, county commissioner (ca. 1868-1870), and community leader. The present school has a bell tower, wooden desks, and potbelly stove. This building is significant because it is the only remaining school in Rockingham County built for Blacks during that time. Reading, writing, and arithmetic were taught at the

Gwynn Colored School

school. Over the many years of its existence, it educated hundreds of Black youths that went on to become outstanding, productive citizens in their community and state. There is an historic site marker erected in front of the school that reads, "Gwynn School House Deeded March 3, 1879." The school house is located **near Shiloh Airport off of Whetstone Circle Road in Shiloh (near Stoneville, NC).**

WARRENTON

Sledge-Hayley House

The Sledge-Hayley House was built between 1852 and 1855 by George R. Sledge, a White merchant and landowner. The house remained in the Sledge family until 1901 when it was sold to Nancy S. Hayley, the wife of Paul F. Hayley, one of the leading Black citizens of Warren County. Mr. Hayley attended Shaw University and later taught school in Warren County. He also served in the General Assembly in 1881 as a representative from Northampton County. He subsequently became chief clerk with the United States Railway Mail Service. Hayley retired in 1920 after rendering thirty-eight years of service. This Greek Revival house has been renovated, but much of the original style remains. The three-story structure has a front hall, two rear rooms, a front room, and stairs, which separate the rooms. This house is located on **the corner of West Franklin and Hayley Street,** also named after Paul Hayley.

Mansfield Thornton House

Mansfield Thornton built his house in the late 1880s. He was born a slave in 1850 in Warrenton and was not freed until 1863. After the Civil War, he moved to Raleigh and found employment with the Internal Revenue Service. He returned to Warrenton and married Mary A. Christmas on December 24, 1873. They had twelve children. Mr. Thornton was the Register of Deeds for Warren County from 1879 to 1900, when he retired.

This two-story, wooden house was of the post-Greek Revival type. It has a hip roof and two brick chimneys. Unlike many homes during this period, this house has many of the late nineteenth century furnishings as well as books and family portraits. This house is located on **the outskirts of Warrenton on Thornton Road.**

All Saints Episcopal Church

All Saints Episcopal Church was built between 1910 and 1914. The church was originally named Thomas Cain Memorial. Church members built it themselves and handmade the gray, stone-like blocks for the structure. For four years, both men and women assisted in the building, determined to complete it, no matter how long it took. When finished, the church also served as a private school for Black children for a number of years. This church, with its lancet, double-windows, and Gothic architecture, has provided spiritual, educational, and social development for Blacks in Warrenton for over seventy-five years. The church is located on **the corner of West Franklin Street and Martin Luther King, Jr. Boulevard.**

METROLINA
REGION

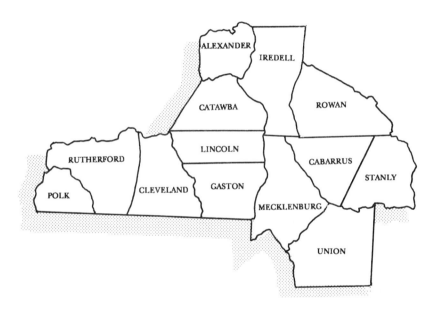

Charlotte   Mount Pleasant
Cleveland   Newell Township
Concord   Salisbury
FranklinTownship   Statesville
Lincolnton   Steele Creek Township

CHARLOTTE

Charlotte-Mecklenburg Afro-American Cultural and Service Center

The Afro-American Cultural and Service Center

The Charlotte-Mecklenburg Afro-American Cultural and Service Center (AACC) was founded in 1974 by Drs. Mary Harper and Bertha Maxwell in direct response to the need for greater community involvement in the cultural and historical heritage of Charlotte's citizens of African descent. The mission of the AACC is to promote, present, and preserve the Afro-American culture and history through various programs and events including:

- Children's Arts Program
- Arts-in-Education Program
- Visual Arts Program
- Guest Artist Performance Series
- Affiliated Artists Program
- Resident Theatre Company

The Old Little Rock A.M.E. Zion Church houses the AACC. The church, founded in 1884, is still a landmark of Charlotte's Black community. The building was purchased by the city of Charlotte in 1979 as part of the city's Urban Renewal Project. However, the Historical Properties Commission designated the church as an historic site, and citizens requested that it become the home of the AACC. The church now symbolizes a people's heritage and pride while strongly identifying with the First Ward, the obsolete Second Ward, and Brooklyn communities. The center has a 180 seat theater and a three hundred seat amphitheater equipped for performances of all kinds. It also has two art galleries, as well as a Resource/Research Center. The AACC is an affiliate of the Charlotte-Mecklenburg Arts and Science Council. Information for this overview was supplied by AACC. It is located at **401 North Myers Street.** It is *open Tuesday-Saturday, 10:00 a.m. to 6:00 p.m., and 1:00 to 5:00 p.m. on Sunday.* ADMISSION IS FREE.

The Mecklenburg Investment Company Building

In May 1921, a number of leading Black citizens formed the Mecklenburg Investment Company (MIC) in Charlotte. They organized the firm in order to obtain enough money from Black shareholders to build an office building in one of Charlotte's Black neighborhoods known as Brooklyn. The founders of MIC intended to rent space in the building to Black professionals and businessmen. Those who purchased stock in the company would share in the profits collected from the rents. The company soon purchased a lot on South Brevard Street in the central city, and the building was completed there in late 1922. At the time of its construction, the three-story, brick commercial building was part of the greater architectural fabric of the Black community of Brooklyn; however, in recent years urban renewal in this section of Charlotte, known as Second Ward, has resulted in the massive demolition of large parts of the community. The Mecklenburg Investment Company Building, Grace A.M.E. Zion Church, and several of the one-story brick buildings between, are the only surviving structures of this once-prosperous neighborhood now characterized by large, modern office buildings, parking lots, and garages. The building is forty-two feet wide and ninety-eight feet deep. The structure stands as an architectural reminder of a significant period in the history of Blacks in the United States. The remodelled building is located at **223 South Brevard Street.**

Johnson C. Smith University

Johnson C. Smith University was founded by Samuel C. Alexander and Willis L. Miller, two White Presbyterian ministers, in 1867, as Biddle Memorial Institute. On the first day of classes there were two teachers and fewer than twelve students . In 1876, the school was granted a charter from the state of North Carolina and the name of the school was changed to Biddle University in honor of Major Henry Biddle. The school adopted its present name in 1923 to honor Johnson C. Smith, who donated funds to the university for the erection of a theological dormitory, a science hall, a teacher's cottage, and a memorial gate.

In 1883, Biddle Memorial Hall was built with bricks made by the students on campus. The dimensions of the new four-story building were ninety-seven feet by sixty-seven feet, with an extension sixty-six feet by forty-five feet, which provided an audience chamber, including a rear balcony, on the west end capable of seating approximately six hundred. For several years, this impressive Romanesque building, with its dramatic tower and elaborate brickwork, provided space for the major offices, classrooms, a reading room, registrar's quarters, a business office, the president's office, and other quarters vital for the execution of the general program.

Biddle Memorial Hall

Besides Biddle Memorial Hall, there are a number of other buildings on Johnson C. Smith University's campus that are of historical significance:

Carter Hall was built in 1896 and is the second oldest building on campus. This two-cone, Tudor building was the gift of Miss Laura Carter of Geneva, New York. It is now used as a men's residence hall.

Carnegie Hall was built in 1911 and was the library until 1968. It was named after its benefactor, Andrew Carnegie, the great philanthropist. Two Greek columns flank the entrance. The building now houses a number of offices.

The **Jane M. Smith Memorial Church** was erected in 1928 and named after its benefactor, Mrs. Jane Smith. This structure with its entrance of four Greek columns and twelve large, oval, stained-glass windows provides space for religious, cultural, and social activities.

There is also **Johnson C. Smith Memorial Hall**, built in 1922; the **Hartley Wood Hall**, the original campus gymnasium, built in 1928; the **George E. Davis Hall**, built in 1923; and the **[Mrs. Johnson C.] Smith Cottage**, the winter home for Mrs. Smith, originally erected in 1928. Johnson C. Smith University is located **off I-85 at 100 Beatties Ford Road.**

The George E. Davis House

The George E. Davis House was built ca. 1895. Dr. Davis was a graduate of Johnson C. Smith as well as its first Black professor. He was also a businessman, civic leader, and agent for the Rosenwald Fund. He died in 1959 at the age of ninety-two. This two-story house was built in a vernacular style. It is located **near Johnson C. Smith University, at 301 Campus Street.**

Grace A.M.E. Zion Church

Grace A.M.E. Zion Church was erected in 1886 under the motto, "God, Religion, and Temperance." The earlier wooden building was replaced in 1902 with the present brick structure. This is a Gothic Revival-style building, with its towers, battlement parapets, and pointed spires of corbeled brick. It also has stone-capped buttresses and projecting ledges of masonry. The church has over the years welcomed some of the major Black community leaders as its members. This church, with its stained-glass windows and Gothic arches, features key stones. It is perhaps the oldest Black church in Charlotte which has continuously functioned in its original location. It is located at **219-233 South Broad Street.**

The Old Mount Carmel Baptist Church

The Old Mount Carmel Baptist Church dates back to 1878 when it was under the leadership of Reverend William H. Davidson. The former wooden building was replaced in 1921 by its present brick structure. This Gothic Revival-style church was built from the plans of Louis Asbury, a leading Charlotte architect. It has been reported that the bricks for the church came from a house that had burned in Myers Park. For many years, Mount Carmel Church provided spiritual and social uplift for Blacks in Biddleville. Mount Carmel Baptist Church moved to a larger building on Tuckaseegee Road in 1977. The Old Mount Carmel Baptist Church building is now the home of Zion Chapel Church of the Living God, located at **529 Campus Street**. The old church is located at **408-416 Campus Street.**

Good Samaritan Hospital

Good Samaritan Hospital was founded in 1891 through the efforts of Mrs. John Wilkes (Jane Renwick Smedberg Wilkes) to serve the Black community. The original hospital was a two-story, brick building. It was the first private hospital for Blacks in North Carolina and one of the first of its kind in the South. Through the years, it has treated thousands of Black patients and fulfilled a medical need that few other facilities took care of. Several modifications were made to the hospital building, including additions. In 1961 it became part of Charlotte Community Hospital. It finally closed in 1981 and is presently being used as the Magnolias Rest Home. It is located at **411 West Hill Street.**

The Excelsior Club

The Excelsior Club was designated an historic landmark by the Charlotte-Mecklenburg Historic Properties Commission because it has the reputation of being the most influential social institution in the Black Community in Charlotte. The original building was erected in 1910 as a Four Square house. In 1944, James "Jimmie" McKee, owner of the club, remodelled the building. Some believe the Excelsior Club is the best example of the Modern Art style in Mecklenburg County. McKee, a leading Black businessman, philanthropist, and political activist in Charlotte, did more renovations in 1952. The owner died in 1985. The club is located **near Johnson C. Smith University at 921 Beatties Ford Road.** *(PRIVATE CLUB)*

Shotgun-Style Houses

Shotgun-style houses were once common residences for Blacks in Charlotte, as well as the greater South in the 1800s and early 1900s. Two such examples have survived. They were built ca. 1898 and originally stood on Bland Street. They were moved behind the Afro-American Cultural Center in 1986. The Center is restoring the houses. Nobody is sure where the name "shotgun" originated. One version suggests that it was because of the long, narrow, one-room deep design. Others contend a shotgun blast fired through the front door would go straight through the house and out the back door. The houses are located at **401 North Myers Street.**

CLEVELAND

Allen Temple Presbyterian Church

Allen Temple Presbyterian Church, according to some records, was an outgrowth of Mount Vernon Presbyterian Church. Allen Temple was built between 1905 and 1906. This wooden building, with its lancet windows and pair of towers, shows a Gothic Revival influence. The walls contain sawnwork ornaments within triangular panels, above rectangular windows. Blacks in the small town of Cleveland have turned to the church for spiritual and social growth for over eighty years. The church is located at **119 Main Street in Cleveland in Rowan County.**

CONCORD

Barber-Scotia College

Barber-Scotia College was founded as Scotia Seminary in January 1867 by Luke Dorland. He was commissioned by the Presbyterian Church, U.S.A., to locate a site and establish an institution for women. Scotia Seminary, incorporated in 1870, immediately attracted much interest throughout the region. It was one of the pioneer institutions in the training of leaders in the fields of education and social service. In 1916, the name of the institution was changed to Scotia Women's College. In 1930, when Barber Memorial College of Anniston, Alabama, was merged with Scotia, the name Barber-Scotia was adopted. Mrs. Margaret M. Barber founded Barber Memorial of Anniston in 1869 as a memorial to her husband.

In March 1931, the College Rating Board of North Carolina gave the institution the standard junior college rating. In 1934, the Southern Association of Colleges and Secondary Schools granted Barber-Scotia the Class "A" rating. Later the college was admitted to membership in the American Association of Junior Colleges. In November 1942, the Board of National Missions took action to expand Barber-Scotia to a four-year accredited college, in order to improve the program of work. In 1945, the first class to be granted

Graves Hall

Faith Hall

the bachelor's degree was graduated. In 1946 the North Carolina Board of Education granted the school the standard Four-Year Rating. This made it possible for their Education graduates to receive the "A" certificate, and therefore be able to teach. In December 1949, the college was rated "Class A" by the Southern Association of Colleges and Secondary Schools and, in December 1955, was admitted to full membership in the Southern Association.

On April 2, 1954, the charter was amended to permit the consideration of applications without regard to race or sex. Barber-Scotia College is owned and operated by the Board of National Missions of the United Presbyterian Church in the United States of America. The campus retains two of its early buildings, Graves Hall (1876 and 1881) and Faith Hall (1891). These buildings have distinctive features of ornamental masonry which is characteristic of Italianate style of architecture. Faith Hall, whose main block and central tower are crowned with mansard roofs, is of the Second Empire style. The college is located at **145 Cabarrus Avenue West.**

The First United Presbyterian Church

The First United Presbyterian Church was erected around 1880 and is the oldest church now in existence in Concord. This church was known at one time as the Concord Presbyterian Church for Colored People. It was later called Westminister Presbyterian Church. Many of the faculty and students at Scotia Seminary (now Barber-Scotia College) attended First United. The United Presbyterian Church, U.S.A. owns and operates Barber-Scotia, and the church is only one block from the college. The Gothic brick church has a gabled nave and a square, three-tiered bell and stair tower. It also has lancet windows and buttresses. The church is part of the Concord Historic District and is located at **127 Cabarrus Avenue West.**

Parkers Chapel A.M.E. Zion Church

Parkers Chapel A.M.E. Zion Church was erected in 1922. The church was originally located in the Silverhill Community of Concord, but the Silverhill congregation later moved to the larger building on Old Charlotte Road. For nearly seventy years, this church has provided spiritual and social enrichment for Blacks in the northeastern part of Concord. This church is located on **Old Charlotte Road.**

Piney Grove A.M.E. Zion Church

Piney Grove A.M.E. Zion Church was founded in 1901 by Wiley Reed and was called Piney Grove Church. It later joined the A.M.E. Zion Conference and subsequently changed its name to Piney Grove A.M.E. Zion Church. This church has provided support for Blacks in Cabarrus County for over ninety years. The church is located at **5 Piney Grove Church Road.**

Reeves Chapel A.M.E. Zion Church

Reeves Chapel A.M.E. Zion Church, founded in the 1890s, was named in honor of Reverend J. A. Reeves, who later served as a Presiding Elder in the A.M.E. Zion Church. Tradition has it that miners exploring Reed Gold Mine built the first church, and that it was also used as a school. The miners donated chairs, lamps, hymn books, and other furniture. The church has spiritually supported Blacks in Cabarrus County for nearly one hundred years. It is located on **Hamby Branch Road.**

FRANKLIN TOWNSHIP

Second Street A.M.E. Zion Church

Second Street A.M.E. Zion Church was built between 1865 and 1867 by the Reverend A. G. Kesler. According to one source, the church was first known as the Zion Society. This small wooden church, with its stained-glass windows and gabled roof, has served the Black community in Franklin Township for over one hundred years.

Unfortunately, the building is vacant and not being used by its members, and as there are so few of them, they do not intend to build another church. Instead, they plan to renovate and preserve it. The church is located on **SR 1946 off of Gheen Road, about 1/3 mile off Hope Hill Road in Rowan County.**

LINCOLNTON

Tucker's Grove Camp Meeting Ground

Tucker's Grove Camp Meeting Ground, founded in the first half of the nineteenth century by the Methodist Episcopal Church, is an early fruit of the Methodist crusade to reach the slave population. The camp was continued after the abolition of slavery and has been operating continuously since 1876 as an A.M.E. Zion camp meeting site under the direction of a board of trustees. Mary E. Tucker donated the oak grove, within which the camp meeting complex is located, to the trustees in 1879. Tucker's Grove Campground, although smaller than its counterparts, is nearly identical in both general plan and structural type to nearby Rock Springs Campground in Lincoln County, and to the other religious camp meeting complexes in western North Carolina. Each, however, was evolved independently through an adaptation of regional, vernacular architecture to fulfill the minimal needs of shelter and assembly.

Tucker's Grove Camp Meeting Ground is near a spring. It contains a central structure called an "arbor," set in the large oak grove. Surrounding the arbor are frame structures called "tents" which form an almost continuous enclosure, roughly square in shape, with alleys at the corners and centers of some rows. Each tent at Tucker's Grove was constructed by an individual family and exhibits minor variations. The typical tent is a one-story, wooden structure with a gabled roof.

The Tucker's Grove Camp Meeting Ground is significant because it is probably the oldest continuously operating Black campground in North Carolina. This campsite provides a rare glimpse at one of the earliest places where Blacks worshipped. The camp meetings fulfilled the need for both safety and fellowship. The meeting ground is located on **SR 1360, near Junction West of Highway NC 73, at Beth Haven Church** Road.

Tucker's Grove Camp Meeting Ground

MOUNT PLEASANT

First Congregational Church

The First Congregational Church is located on a one and three-tenths acre lot in the town of Mount Pleasant. The church is the

First Congregational Church

second house of worship for a congregation which was formally organized in 1900 under the leadership of J. C. McClean. McClean was a missionary who had moved to Mount Pleasant from Guilford County. The church is also associated with Robert Franklin Lynn, a deacon and local stonemason. Lynn, with the help of Calvin Bost, erected the Congregational Church in 1921, after the 1906 building was destroyed by fire in 1918.

The church retains many of its original exterior features. The 1923 brick flue has been replaced with a modern counterpart and is located on the north side of the nave. The concrete buildings, found directly behind the church and almost flush to the rear wall of the "service room," were added in 1979.   The First Congregational Church has a long local history, and is an established and respected institution in the Black community.   The church is a visible testament of the Black population's history in Mount Pleasant, and the contribution of the New England-based Congregational Church as they expanded their missionary efforts to include and serve those members of the population which the church fought so hard to free.   The church is located at **the northeast corner junction of Wade and C Streets.**

NEWELL TOWNSHIP

Newell School

Newell School was built for Black youths between 1928 and 1929 with financial support from Julius Rosenwald.   The Torrence Grove A.M.E. Zion Church also helped raise money for the school building. Newell School had three classrooms and an "industrial room," where cooking, sewing, and woodwork were taught.   The school also had three chimneys, a double-door entrance, and fourteen-foot ceilings. It is well-preserved.   Over the years, the school has provided one of the centers of Black social and spiritual life in Newell and Crab Orchard Townships.   Presently the building is being restored.   Currently, Silverset Lodge #327, Free and Accepted Masons, a Black Masonic Organization, is using the building for a lodge hall.   The school building is located **off Old Concord Road on Torrence Grove Church Road, on the southwest edge of Newell.**

SALISBURY

Livingstone College

Livingstone College was founded in 1879 by Joseph Charles Price. The college has been designated as an historic district. In addition to most of the buildings on campus, there are also a number of nearby houses and buildings included in the historic district. Livingstone College is located in the **600 block of West Monroe Street.** Livingstone College Historic District includes the following places:

Moore's Chapel at **500 Partee Street,** is a brick cross-gable chapel, constructed about 1905, which served as a place of worship for much of the Livingstone community.

Madison-Miller House, at **1008 West Monroe,** is a two-story Victorian frame house which was built about 1904 as an A.M.E. Zion clergyman's residence.

At **1002 West Monroe,** there is an interesting two-story Victorian frame house.

Crittenden House, at **928 West Monroe,** is a one and one-half-story, wooden bungalow built about 1916 as a faculty residence.

Hannum House is located at **924 West Monroe.** It is a two-story Victorian frame house built in 1904 as a faculty residence.

Trent House, at **918 West Monroe,** is a one and one-half-story frame house built in 1928 as a residence for the college president.

Wallace-Hall House is found at **912 West Monroe.** It is a one and one-half-story, wooden bungalow built in 1915 for a local dentist. It later became a faculty residence.

Price House, at **828 West Monroe,** is a two-story brick Victorian house built in 1884 for the college founder and president.

Joseph C. Price

Dancy House is located at **814 West Monroe.** It is a two-story Victorian frame house built in 1890 for the A.M.E. Zion clergyman, editor, and college instructor.

At **806-810 West Monroe,** there is a two-story, brick residence.

Harris House, at **802 West Monroe,** is a two-story Victorian frame house built in 1889 to be used as a faculty residence.

At **427 South West Street,** there is a two-story L-shaped apartment building.

Stevenson House, at **714 West Monroe,** is a two-story Victorian frame house built about 1904 as a faculty residence.

Aggrey House, located at **700 West Monroe,** is a two-story Victorian frame house built in 1912 for Professor Aggrey of Africa.

Ballard Hall is a two-story brick classroom building constructed in 1887.

Dodge Hall is a three-story brick building built for dormitory and classroom space in 1886.

Carnegie Library, a two-story brick structure with classical portico, was built in 1908, with later additions.

Goler Hall, a three-story brick building, was built in 1917 as a women's dormitory, dining hall, and post office facility.

Hood Building is a two-story brick structure built in 1910 to house the Hood Theological Seminary.

Price Memorial Building, a two-story brick building, was constructed in 1930 and used until 1943 to house administrative functions.

An athletic marker was erected in 1956 to commemorate the first Black intercollegiate football game in 1892.

The Tomb of Joseph Charles Price was erected at his grave in 1923.

James E. Varick Auditorium is a brick auditorium constructed in 1963.

S. E. Duncan Building, a brick classroom building, was completed in 1968.

The Harriet Tubman Building is a brick classroom building dedicated in 1969.

Bishop and Mrs. William J. Walls donated and dedicated the **Walls Heritage House** in February of 1969. This brick building is Livingstone College's center for studies on African and African-American life and literature. It has hundreds of books, newspapers, photographs, and documents on various aspects of African-American history.

The college also has **The Poets and Dreamers Garden**, which is said to be the only one of its kind in the United States. This garden was dedicated on February 12, 1967 and is located around Price's mausoleum. At one time or another, it has contained a Biblical Garden; Phyllis Wheatley Fountain; William Shakespeare Garden; Samuel E. Duncan Sundial; David Livingstone Walk; Sue Bailey Thurman Pool; International Garden; Jennie Smallwood Price Azalea Trail; Samuel E. Duncan and John H. Nicholson Birdbath; Bronze Busts of Lorraine Hansberry, Langston Hughes and William Shakespeare; the Calbert California Gardens, and dedicated trees and shrubbery.

Soldier's Memorial A.M.E. Zion Church

Soldier's Memorial A.M.E. Zion Church was established by Reverends William Pitts and A. G. Kessler in 1865 as Zion Society. One local tradition states it was given its name, Soldier's Memorial, in memory of the Union soldiers who freed the Southern slaves. The earlier building was replaced by the present one, constructed between 1910 and 1913. Soldiers Memorial A.M.E. Zion has been connected with Livingstone College since the 1880s. Many of its faculty and students have been members of this church. The church has twin buttressed towers, and exhibits the Romanesque Revival style. It also has lancet arched, stained-glass windows. Soldiers Memorial is constructed in red brick with stone trim, has a gable front, and is ornamented with crenulated parapets. The church has been an important part of the Black community for many years. It is located at **306 North Church Street.**

Mt. Zion Baptist Church

The Mt. Zion Baptist Church was organized in 1867. The present church was built in 1907 on land purchased by the congregation in 1893. Mt. Zion was one of a number of congregations founded by Harry Cowan (1810-1904), a man born into slavery who was to become one of the leaders of the Black Baptist church in North Carolina. Mt. Zion is believed to be the second Black Baptist church in the county. Reverend Cowan was pastor of the congregation from 1867 until 1891. Fisher Robert Mason was pastor from 1902 until 1929, the period which saw the construction of the present building. By 1920,

Mt. Zion Baptist Church

a large, brick-veneered educational wing/manse was added to the structure. This wing housed an important school from 1920 until 1928, under the leadership of Mrs. Fannie Mason. The Sunshine School offered religious and academic training for grades one through six at a time when such schooling was not readily available for young Blacks. During Mason's tenure, Mt. Zion became one of the largest and most influential Black churches in Salisbury and Rowan County. It maintained that position for many years. The brick veneer was probably added to the sanctuary in the late 1920s. Mount Zion Baptist Church embodies, on a modest scale, the distinctive characteristics of the late Gothic Revival style in church architecture. The church is located on **White Road in Salisbury.**

STATESVILLE

Mt. Pleasant Center Street A.M.E. Zion Church

Mt. Pleasant Center Street A.M.E. Zion Church was constructed in 1903 by Reverend S. S. Murdock. It is the oldest structure associated with a Black congregation in Statesville. The Methodist congregation, established as Mt. Pleasant ca. 1868, was one of many which formed its own church within the Black community soon after the Civil War. The Gothic Revival style of the building, executed in intricate corbeled, paneled, and molded brickwork, is characteristic of the substantial churches built for many Black congregations as they gained permanence and prosperity. The church is located at **537 South Center Street**.

STEELE CREEK TOWNSHIP

McClintock School

McClintock School was built in 1922 with the financial assistance of Julius Rosenwald. The McClintock Presbyterian Church also supported the school financially, which was built for Black youths. It opened in October 1922. Unlike some other "Rosenwald Colored" Schools, McClintock had three classrooms, an industrial room, and a cloak room. It has a high, hipped roof, a wide porch, and double front doors. Many consider the McClintock School to be the best preserved Rosenwald School in Mecklenburg County. Over the years, the school, along with the local church, was the center of the social and political life of Blacks in Steele Creek Township. It is now being preserved by the McClintock Presbyterian Church. The school is located on **Erwin Road, West of NC 49, near Carowinds.**

WESTERN REGION

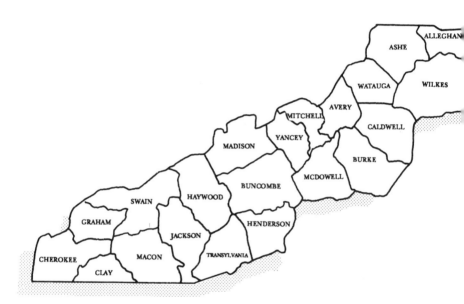

Asheville

Morganton

An 1893 photograph of the Young Men's Institute

ASHEVILLE

The Young Men's Institute

The Young Men's Institute (YMI) building was constructed between the years 1891 and 1892, as a community center for the Black citizens of Asheville. Founded by George Vanderbilt, who was building a great estate near Asheville at the time, the Young Men's Institute was intended to serve not only Asheville's Black community but also the many Black workers involved in the construction of Biltmore. The two-story pebbledash and brick building was designed by Richard Sharp Smith, a native of England who served as resident and supervising architect for Biltmore under Richard Morris Hunt.

The building was nearly completed on February 12, 1892, when the organizational meeting of the Young Men's Institute was held. The electric lights had yet to be installed, and the concrete pavement around the building, to be poured. The building was described in the Asheville Daily Citizen as "one of the handsomest in Asheville." The Young Men's Institute apparently thrived in its early days, serving as a meeting place and true community center. It offered a kindergarten, a gymnasium, and even bathing facilities, where over two thousand baths were taken in one year. Among the most popular events were the Sunday afternoon song services. The Young Men's Institute also extended its facilities to the Black churches, public schools, and civic organizations, which held their entertainments in the YMI hall. The early success of the YMI is largely attributed to its large membership roster. All of the Black men working on the Biltmore estate were required to purchase a YMI membership. But, as work at Biltmore decreased and men fell to unemployment, financial difficulties arose for the Institute. In 1905, George Vanderbilt offered to sell the YMI for ten thousand dollars to its board of trustees if they could raise the amount in six months. Even though this was a tremendous undertaking for the Black community, they raised the money and the property was transferred to the Young Men's Institute, Inc.

The Institute flourished for nearly thirty years after the transaction until the Great Depression took its toll. Then the building fell into disrepair and was closed. The YMI was largely inactive during the early 1940s because of the war and inadequate financial support. When it became active again, most of its programs were to raise money for the building's repairs. In 1946, the YMI was sold again. This time the property was transferred to the Market Street Branch YMCA for its primary use as a recreational facility. The 1960s began a gradual deterioration of the Market and Eagle Streets neighborhood. Desegregation, and other social and political changes, prompted the relocation of several homes and businesses from the area, thus extinguishing one of Asheville's most established neighborhoods. Unable to maintain its upkeep, the Market Street Branch YMCA (YMI) closed in 1976 and, after failing to meet city codes in 1977, the building was condemned. In that same year, the efforts of Mr. Johnny Baxter rewarded the YMI with placement on the National Register of Historic Places. Realizing that they could not allow a valued landmark to be destroyed, other members of the Black community began a project to regain ownership, restore the building, and initiate programs reflecting its traditions. This project was led by representatives from nine of Asheville's Black churches which constituted the Friendship Nursing Home. The Friendship Board voted to amend the charter, and change the name to the YMI Cultural Center, Inc. (YMICC). The YMICC inherited thirty-one thousand dollars from the Friendship and purchased the building in September of 1980. One year later, a $750,000 Capital Funds Drive was launched to renovate the building. Charitable foundations, government agencies, social organizations, churches, and individual donors contributed to the restoration of the YMI. The quality of the project was recognized in 1982 when the YMICC received the Stedman Incentive

Award from the Historic Preservation Society of North Carolina. Renovations were completed in August of 1988.

Today, the elegant three-story structure contains eighteen thousand square feet of space which includes 7,500 square feet of museum/exhibit space. The gymnasium has been converted into a 350 seat auditorium. In addition to presenting those programs sponsored by the YMICC, the auditorium and other designated spaces are available for rent by the community. With programs in cultural arts, community education, and economic development, the YMI Cultural Center sets out to empower the community's poor and minority citizens through self-help programs or "practices." The building's very existence and development against the odds, represents determination, strength in community, and a will to survive. Its rebirth, from what seemed mere skeletal remains, should spark the energy to face new struggles in a new era. Most of this information was supplied by the YMI Cultural Center, Inc. The YMI Cultural Center is located at **39 South Market Street** and is *open Monday-Friday, 9:00 a.m. - 5:00 p.m.* Phone (704) 252-4614.

St. Matthias Episcopal Church

The St. Matthias Episcopal Church stands on the western slope of Beaucatcher Mountain in Asheville's "East End," the historic Black neighborhood of the town. The church is considered by many to be one of the finest churches ever built for a Black congregation in North Carolina. The handsome Gothic-style brick structure, with elaborate interior woodwork, houses the oldest congregation of Black Episcopalians in the western part of the state. First known as Trinity Chapel, it was founded for the newly freed slaves of the area in 1865 by Jarvis Buxton, a noted Episcopal rector. Buxton had organized the first Episcopal congregation for free Blacks in North Carolina in Fayetteville in 1832. Trinity Chapel flourished under various leaders

and, by the end of the nineteenth century, they needed a new building to serve the growing congregation. Bishop Joseph Blount
Cheshire laid the cornerstone of the present structure in February
1894; the building was completed in 1896. The name of the church
changed to St. Matthias. St. Matthias maintained its influence into
the twentieth century, and has aided in the formation of several Black
Episcopal churches in the Diocese of western North Carolina.

The church is of a simple Gothic character. It is built on a

St. Matthias Episcopal Church

cruciform plan, with a gable-roofed nave on an east-west axis which
intersects the transepts and terminates on the east end in a semi-
hexagonal apse. A small gable-roofed chapel is attached to the
southeast corner of the south transept. The brick is laid in one-to-five
common bond, with the darker rows of headers giving a horizontal
texture to the surface of the building on every face.

The nave is four bays deep, with the division marked by buttresses. A lancet-arch window, set on a stone sill and topped by a brick hoodmold, is centered on each bay. Similar windows flank the entrance of the three bay nave. The double-leaf main entrance is set in a lancet surround of stone voussoirs. Though the doors are modern replacements, the wooden tympanum above them is original. Above the entrance is a large rose window of stained glass in a cinquefoil pattern; centered above this in the peak of the gable is a small lancet-arch, louvered ventilator with a wooden cross superimposed on it. A finial in the shape of a cross rises from the peak of the gable. The Gothic-style building with its interior woodwork rivals any of its type built by either race in the late nineteenth century.

The building is a landmark in Asheville's Black history. The church is located on **Valley Street between Grail Street and East Beaumont Street.**

MORGANTON

Gaston Chapel

The nucleus of Gaston Chapel was an outgrowth of the African Methodist Episcopal congregation founded in Morganton around 1872. Gaston Chapel, which took its name from Reverend Moses Gaston, an early Black minister in Burke County (1863-66), was established as a separate entity by 1881. At the same time, Slades Chapel A.M.E. Zion Church also split from the former congregation and built its own house of worship on the southeast side of East Union Street, across from Gaston Chapel. Members of Gaston Chapel worshipped in a smaller wooden church northwest of the present structure until the new church was completed ca. 1905. Some believe land for both the earlier and present structures was sold to the Methodist Episcopal Colored Church by Tod R. Caldwell, a Morganton native and governor of North Carolina between 1872 and 1874.

Gaston Chapel is the oldest existing and first substantial Black church structure in Burke County. The brick building, a pared-down interpretation of turn-of-the-century, ecclesiastical Gothic architecture with some Romanesque influences, was largely erected by congregation members and retains most of its original integrity. The

Gaston Chapel

basic design is modeled after White churches constructed in the same mode in Burke County during the 1890s. The history of Gaston Chapel from its inception is tied to the initial organization of Burke County Blacks into religious bodies, following their expulsion from established churches after the Civil War. The congregation has always been a vital component of the Black community in Morganton, and presently has the largest membership of any African Methodist Episcopal church in the county. The church is located at **100 Bouchelle Street.**

PART TWO

HIGHWAY
HISTORICAL
MARKERS

INTRODUCTION

Of the more than thirteen hundred state and private markers erected across North Carolina, forty-six are related to Blacks. These markers are significant because they tell us a great deal about the accomplishments of Black North Carolinians. The first highway marker to honor a Black person was erected for John Chavis in 1938, more than fifty-two years ago. Since that time, forty-five more markers concerning Blacks have been erected. Of these markers, made of cast aluminum and mounted on seven or ten-foot posts, twenty-three honor Black individuals, fifteen concern educational institutions, two honor churches, two relate to events, one honors a town, one honors a community, one recognizes an orphanage, and one honors Siamese twins. Joseph Charles Price is the only Black individual to have two markers erected in his honor. One is located in Elizabeth City, his birthplace, and the other one is located in Salisbury, near where he founded Livingstone College and lived.

These markers are important not only because they honor Blacks and their achievements, but also because these markers identify the community in which they lived. This writer hopes these markers not only spark curiosity leading to further study of and appreciation for the historical development of the region, but that others will identify and nominate worthy individuals, institutions, buildings, and events to the Highway Historical Marker Advisory Committee. Individuals wishing to report missing or damaged markers or to propose a subject for a new marker should address correspondence to: Research Supervisor, Division of Archives and History, 109 East Jones Street, Raleigh, North Carolina 27601-2807. The latest (1990) *Guide of North Carolina Historical Markers* is also published by the Division of Archives and History at the above address.

NORTHEAST REGION

Bricks

Elizabeth City

Manteo

Princeville

Rocky Mount

Tarboro

Winton

BRICKS

BRICK SCHOOL
:st. for blacks in 1895
hrough philanthropy
•f Mrs. Joseph K. Brick:
)ecame junior college
n 1926. Closed. 1933.
3uildings stood here.

In 1895, Julia E. Brick (Mrs. Joseph K. Brick), a White philanthropist from Brooklyn, New York, deeded 1,105 1/2 acres of land to the American Missionary Association (AMA) for ten thousand dollars. She also gave the association six thousand dollars for the first building. The AMA established the **Joseph Keasby Brick Agricultural, Industrial and Normal School** in 1895. When Mrs. Brick died, she also bequeathed a large sum of money to the school. Thomas Sewell Inborden, a Black man and 1891 graduate of Fisk University, helped complete the first building and later became principal of the school. He held this position for thirty-one years, until 1925. He advocated "better homes, better farms, better schools and better churches" for Blacks. In its early years, the school provided elementary and high school education for Black students. Much emphasis was placed on industrial education. The school raised all of the food for the students and was nearly self-sufficient. In 1926, it became a junior college and was one of the four Black colleges in the South accredited by the Association of Colleges and Secondary Schools. It was considered one of the best Negro schools of its kind in the South.

The school was maintained by tuition and board from the students as well as an annual appropriation from the American Missionary Association. In the 1931-1932 school year, there were student applications from nineteen states and one foreign country. In 1933, because of the Great Depression and the students' inability to pay their school bills, the American Missionary Association stopped supporting the college and sold it to the county for one dollar to be used as a county training school. For nearly forty years, the school graduated thousands of students, and many of them became teachers, dentists, businessmen, and outstanding farmers. The marker for the school is located on **US 301 at Bricks in Edgecombe County.**

ELIZABETH CITY

House Bill 383 in the North Carolina General Assembly, to establish Elizabeth City State University, was introduced on March 3, 1891, by Hugh Cale, a Black representative from Pasquotank County. Initially, the institution was created by law as a normal school for the specific purpose of "teaching and training teachers" of the Black race "to teach in the common schools" of North Carolina. It was named State Colored Normal School and began operation on January 4, 1892, with a budget of nine hundred dollars, however, neither a building nor site was designated. The citizens of Elizabeth City and Peter Weddick Moore, who had been appointed principal of the school, purchased the Rooks Turner Building. The school opened with two faculty members and twenty-three students.

In 1899, the institution survived a statewide effort to consolidate normal schools and, during the same year, began its first summer session. The school moved to its present and permanent location on September 9, 1912. Between 1891 and 1928, the curriculum was expanded from elementary and secondary school level courses to two-year "normal" courses under the leadership of Peter W. Moore.

The institution was elevated from a two-year to a four-year teachers' college in 1937, and its name was officially changed to Elizabeth City State Teachers College by an Act of the North Carolina

General Assembly as of March 30, 1939. In addition to its original purpose, a second purpose was added: the training of elementary school principals for rural and city schools. Thus, the first bachelor of science degrees, in elementary education, were awarded by the college to twenty-six graduates in May 1939.

Peter W. Moore

The name of the institution was officially changed from **Elizabeth City State Teachers College** to Elizabeth City State College by an act of the North Carolina General Assembly in 1963, but it remained a predominantly teacher-training institution. In 1972, the name was once again changed to Elizabeth City State University, and it was made one of the sixteen constituent universities of The University of North Carolina. Over its one hundred year history, Elizabeth City State University graduates have made significant contributions in the fields of education, medicine, science, religion, law, and other professions. The institution's marker is located on **NC 34 in Elizabeth City, Pasquotank County.**

JOSEPH C. PRICE
(1854-1893)

Negro orator and teacher.
A founder and president
of Livingstone College.
Born in Elizabeth City.
House was 2 miles S.

Joseph Charles Price was born a free Black in Elizabeth City, North Carolina on February 10, 1854. In 1863, Price and his mother moved to New Bern. While there, he attended St. Cyprian Episcopal School. Since he wanted to advance his education, in 1873, he entered Shaw University. He stayed only a short while and transferred to Lincoln University in Pennsylvania, graduating valedictorian of his class in 1879 with an A.B. degree in Theology. In 1881, Price, along with Bishop James Walker Hood and others, attended the Methodist Ecumenical Conference in London, England. After the conference, Price stayed in England for a year and raised nearly ten thousand dollars for Zion Wesley Institute, later to become Livingstone College. In 1882, Price returned to Salisbury and was elected president of Zion Wesley Institute. It was Price's fund-raising efforts that resulted in the founding of the institute, and it was at his urging that the Board of Bishops voted to change the name to Livingstone College.

Joseph Charles Price was more than a college president and world-renowned orator; he was also an acknowledged national leader. In 1890, he was elected president of the two Black national conventions--the Afro-American League and the National Protective Association. During the same year, Price was also selected as one of "The Ten Greatest Negroes Who Ever Lived" in a poll taken by *The* Indianapolis Freedman.

During his short life, Joseph Charles Price was offered many positions which he turned down. He could have been a bishop, congressman, United States Minister Plenipotentiary to Liberia, and businessman. His one goal was to build Livingstone College into a first-rate liberal arts institution. He died of Bright's disease on October 25, 1893, at age thirty-nine. Joseph Charles Price was an educator, internationally known orator, minister, Pan-Africanist, women's rights advocate, founder of a college, and leader of his people. His marker is located on **NC 34 (Water Street) in Elizabeth City, Pasquotank County.**

MANTEO

ANDREW CARTWRIGHT

Agent of the American Colonization Society in Liberia, founded the A.M.E. Zion churches in Albemarle area. His first church, 1865, near here.

Andrew Cartwright was born in 1837 in either Elizabeth City or Manteo, North Carolina. Some writers state he was born into slavery. Others claim he was freeborn. He was apparently taught to read and write by White people in the area. He subsequently converted to Christianity and gave his life to Christ. In 1860, he was ordained a minister in the A.M.E. Zion Church. Cartwright was credited with being the founder of twelve churches between 1865 and 1876 in the Albemarle section of the state. Some of the churches he founded include: Cartwright Memorial Church, located on Roanoke Island; Good Hope A.M.E. Zion Church, Currituck County; Pilgrim Journey, Moyock, North Carolina; Parkville A.M.E. Zion Church at Indian Town, Camden County; the New McBride Church at South Mills, North Carolina; and a host of churches in Pasquotank and Perquimans Counties as well as churches in Plymouth, Jamesville, Macedonia, and Bethel. While in North Carolina, he was an agent for the American Colonization Society. Many of the churches that he established in that area are still in operation today.

Andrew Cartwright

Another one of Reverend Cartwright's achievements was a voyage to Liberia, Africa in 1876, where he established churches in Brewerville, Clay Ashland, and Antherton, Liberia. His trip was paid for by the American Colonization Society. He also built churches in Ghana and Nigeria. Reverend Cartwright

was the first missionary to go to Liberia, and the first to establish the
A.M.E. Zion Church in both West Africa and America. The Reverend
Andrew Cartwright, preacher, missionary, evangelist, educator, and
founder of churches, died in 1903 in Brewerville, Liberia, at age
sixty-eight. His marker is located on **NC 345 at US 64/264, southeast
of Manteo in Dare County.**

PRINCEVILLE

According to a report on the history of Princeville, at the close of the Civil War, Union
troops occupied the Tarboro area. During those
weeks, many of the former slaves in Edgecombe
and surrounding counties left their plantations
and came to the Federals' encampment seeking
freedom and protection. The future faced by the mostly illiterate,
unskilled, penniless freedmen was uncertain and bleak. They con-
gregated around the Union troops bivouacked on the south side of
the Tar River below Tarboro. Although it was the soldiers' policy to
advise the emancipated slaves to return to the plantations and work
for their old masters, a sizable number of Blacks remained encamped
at the site after the troops departed. These freedmen called their new
village **Freedom Hill** (sometimes known as Liberty Hill). They
adopted the name from a nearby hill or knoll from which Northern
soldiers had addressed the former slaves–telling them that the Union
victory in the war made them free men. The knoll where the soldiers
made their speeches was on the west side of Old Sparta Road near
what is now the area's major traffic intersection.

The freedmen who remained encamped on the river soon erected
crude shanties. White landowners made no effort to evict them, since
the land was so swampy as to be otherwise useless. In fact, there is

some evidence that the "squatters" were encouraged to remain at the site and thus keep their distance from the White community in Tarboro. In the 1870s, the land did change hands and Blacks began acquiring lots. One of the buyers was Turner Prince (1843-1912), a carpenter for whom the community was renamed upon its incorporation in 1885, according to a historical sketch of Princeville. The town's economy improved in the late nineteenth and early twentieth centuries with the proliferation of Black-owned businesses. The rise of White supremacy brought a serious threat to Princeville's continued existence as a Black town. Calls mounted for its dissolution, but the residents resisted. Today Princeville remains a cohesive Black community with a heritage unique among North Carolina towns. Princeville was the first Black community incorporated in the state of North Carolina. Princeville itself lays claim to being the "oldest city chartered by Blacks in America," and, in fact, uses those words on its official stationery. The marker for the town is located on **US 64 Business at US 258 in Princeville, Edgecombe County.**

ROCKY MOUNT

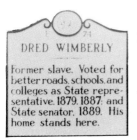

Dred Wimberly was born a slave in 1849 in Edgecombe County, North Carolina. Little is known about his early childhood except that he was the property of James S. Battle of Edgecombe County. In 1879, he was elected a representative to the North Carolina General Assembly. He was elected again in 1887, and two years later, he became state senator to the General Assembly. Wimberly served one term. Legend has it that he cast the deciding vote to save the University of North Carolina at Chapel Hill from financial ruin. The vote was taken to grant fifteen thousand dollars to the University of North

Carolina against the opposition of some legislators who felt that the state could not afford such a large appropriation to a university. The following is Mr. Wimberly's account of what happened:

> "I voted for Dr. (Kemp P.) Battle's appropriation because Dr. Battle had said voting for the university would help everybody. It might somehow help the colored folks, too. We wanted some schooling, and we might want somebody to vote for us sometimes."

Dred Wimberly

While in the General Assembly, Wimberly also supported a bill to establish normal schools and a bill to help improve and rebuild roads damaged during the Civil War.

In 1900, Mr. Wimberly was a delegate to the Republican National Convention and helped nominate Theodore Roosevelt as vice-president. In 1902 he returned to Rocky Mount with his wife and eighteen children. He died in 1937 at age eighty-eight. Dred Wimberly was an honest man, politician, state representative, state senator, family man, supporter of education, and a Republican. His marker is located on **US 64 (Raleigh Street) in Rocky Mount, Edgecombe County.**

TARBORO

John Campbell Dancy was born May 8, 1857, in Tarboro, North Carolina. He attended the public schools in that town and later studied at Howard University. During his youth, Dancy worked as a typesetter for the Tarboro Southerner. In the 1870s, he was principal of a Black grade school in Tarboro. Dancy was also editor of the *North Carolina Sentinel.* In 1882, Dancy was elected president of a Black temperance convention that met in Goldsboro. Between 1880 and 1890, he was chief secretary of the State Republican Convention. In 1891, Dancy served as Collector of Customs in Wilmington at a salary of approximately four thousand dollars per year, about one thousand more than the annual salary of the state governor. He held this position until 1893.

In 1885, Dancy was elected editor of the A.M.E. Zion Church's official organ, The Star of Zion. He moved to Salisbury, where it was being published, and remained in that position for seven years. In 1892, Dancy was elected editor of the A.M.E. Zion Quarterly Review, a publication he edited until 1910. Dancy continued to offer his services to the church during which, in 1912, he was elected Corresponding Secretary of the Church Extension Department.

John Dancy

At various times during his life, John C. Dancy held a number of positions, including one in the Treasury Department, Register of Deeds, Recorder of Deeds, trustee of Livingstone College, and board member of the Warren C. Coleman Manufacturing Company. He died April 13, 1920, at age sixty-three. John Campbell Dancy was a typesetter, orator, statesman, newspaperman, editor, churchman, Odd Fellow, Mason, public official, politician, and businessman. His marker is located on **US 64 Business (Main Street) at St. James Street in Tarboro, Edgecombe County.**

WINTON

A 58

CHOWAN ACADEMY

Founded for Negroes. 1886.
by C. S. Brown, pastor
of the Pleasant Plains
Baptist Church. Since
1937, the Calvin Scott
Brown High School.

Calvin Scott Brown was born in 1859 in Salisbury, North Carolina, but little is known of Brown's early childhood. He did, however, graduate from Shaw University in 1886. Brown came to Hertford County in 1883 as pastor of Pleasant Baptist Church, and in 1886, started **Chowan Academy**. He received financial support from both Blacks and Whites. Five acres of land for the school was donated by Levi C. Brown, Sr. The first building on campus was three stories high and contained classrooms, a printing shop, a chapel, and residence hall. Students paid a fee of $1.75 a week. The first year, there were thirty-five boarding students and eighty-five day students. The school term was six months, and there were four faculty members. In 1893, Miss Annie Walden became the first graduate of Chowan Academy. Over the years the school continued to receive more students and more financial support, especially from wealthy Whites in both the North and South. At one time, Mr. Waters, a White benefactor from New York, donated eight thousand dollars. In 1893, the academy changed its name to Waters Normal Institute in honor of its benefactor.

The school became so successful that several of the Black schools in the county closed because they could not compete with the fund-raising skills of Waters Normal. In 1922, however, the school could not meet all of its financial needs, and Reverend Brown asked the County Board of Education to take over the school and its administration. The county took over the school and changed its name to the Hertford County Training School. In 1924, the name was changed again to Waters Training School and the state of North Carolina became responsible for the school's debts. Dr. Brown remained a teacher there until his death in 1936. He had been associated with that school for more than fifty years. In 1937, the name was changed to the Calvin Scott Brown High School. Over the years, the school

graduated many Black students who were inspired by Dr. Brown's methods and philosophy. Many students went on to become doctors, lawyers, dentists, ministers, judges and a host of other professions. The Chowan Academy marker is located on **Main Street in Winton in Hertford County.**

C.S. Brown

A turn-of-the-century publicity photograph

CENTRAL COASTAL REGION

James City
New Bern

JAMES CITY

JAMES CITY
Community founded here
in 1863 as resettlement
camp for freed slaves.
Named for Horace James,
Union Army chaplain.

James City, North Carolina was named in honor of Horace James, a Chaplain in the Union Army during the Civil War. In 1862, the Union Army seized New Bern and thousands of slaves sought freedom behind the Union lines. In 1863, Chaplain James established a camp for the exslaves which came to be called the Trent River Camp, since it was located a few miles from New Bern across Trent River. The camp was later administered by the Freedman's Bureau. Mr. James worked for the bureau, and made a significant impact upon the settlement. Because of his work with the freedmen the settlement was named James City.

Over the years, James City was a strong, cohesive community which was the essence of Black political, social, and economic self-reliance. Although the majority of the settlers were farmers, they were proud to own their own land. Gradually, residents began to seek other economic opportunities. Many left to move to New Bern and other towns outside of the area. James City is a good example of Black self-sufficiency from 1863 to present. The marker for the town is located on **US 70 Bypass at James City, Craven County.**

NEW BERN

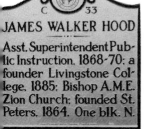

JAMES WALKER HOOD
Asst. Superintendent Public Instruction, 1868-70; a founder Livingstone College, 1885; Bishop A.M.E. Zion Church; founded St. Peters, 1864. One blk. N.

James Walker Hood was born May 30, 1831, on a farm in Chester County, Pennsylvania. His father, Levi Hood, was a Methodist minister. James had little formal education during his childhood, and was mainly self-taught. At an early age he was baptized. In 1856, he was licensed to preach by the A.M.E. Zion Church in New York. Between 1859 and 1863, he held a number of pastoral positions in the North. In 1863, Reverend Hood was sent to North Carolina as a missionary. A year later, he helped found the North Carolina Conference. In 1865, Reverend Hood established St. Peter's Church in New Bern, North Carolina. This became the first A.M.E. Zion Church in the South.

In October, 1865, James Walker Hood was elected president of the Convention of Blacks, held in Raleigh. This was the first statewide Black political convention. Three years later, he attended the North Carolina State Constitutional Convention. He was a strong advocator of public education for all people, especially for Blacks. Reverend Hood served as the first Black Assistant Superintendent of Education in North Carolina between 1868 and 1871. His primary responsibility was founding and supervising Black schools. Before

James Hood

Hood was elected a bishop in the A.M.E. Zion church in 1872, he held a number of other positions: Magistrate, Deputy Collector of Customs, Assistant Superintendent of the Freedman's Bureau in North Carolina, and North Carolina's First Grand Master of the Masons. He also participated in the temperance movement in North Carolina. Hood was one of the founders of Livingstone College and served as chairman of the college's Board of Trustees for more than thirty years.

Besides being a minister and educator, he was also the author of five books and numerous articles. This is remarkable, given the fact that he had little formal education. The books were: *The Negro in the Christian Pulpit* (1884); *One Hundred Years of the African Methodist Episcopal Zion Church* (1895); *The Plan of the Apocalypse* (1900); *Sermons by...*(1908); and *Sketch of the Early History of African Methodist Episcopal Zion Church* (1914).

Bishop Hood died in Fayetteville, North Carolina, on October 30, 1918, at age eighty-five, and was buried in that city after his funeral at Evans Chapel. James Walker Hood was a minister, educator, founder of churches and schools, politician, bishop, and Grand Master of the Masons. His marker is erected on **US 70 Business (Broad Street) at George Street in New Bern, Craven County.**

George Henry White was born December 18, 1852, in the town of Rosindale in Bladen County, North Carolina. He attended public schools in that area and graduated from Howard University in 1877. In 1878, White became principal of the Colored State Normal School in Oxford. In 1879, he passed the bar and began practicing law in New Bern. One year later, he was elected from Craven County to be a representative to the North Carolina General Assembly. In 1884, he served as a senator in the General Assembly. Between 1886 and 1894, White was Solicitor and Prosecuting Attorney for the Second Judicial District of

George White

North Carolina. White was elected to the United States House of Representatives in both 1896 and 1898, from the Second Congressional District, the so-called "Black Second." While in Congress, he supported all bills that were pro-Black. White proposed a bill that would require the federal government to appropriate one million dollars to reimburse depositors (who were mostly Black) who had lost their savings through the failure of the Freedman's Saving and Trust Company. The bill passed. White "from time to time displayed partisanship, race consciousness, and nonpartisanship." White did not seek re-election in 1902, thereby being the last Black elected to Congress until 1930.

White returned to North Carolina and practiced law. He was also a banker. White died December 28, 1918, at age sixty-six. George Henry White was a teacher, lawyer, politician, congressman, banker, churchman, and racial spokesman. His marker is located on **US 70 Business (Broad Street) at Metcalf Street in New Bern, Craven County.**

CAPE FEAR REGION

Whiteville
Wilmington

WHITEVILLE

Mille-Christine were Black Siamese twin slaves born on July 11, 1851, in Whiteville, North Carolina, to Jacob and Monemia, and were the property of Jabe McCoy. The twins were united at the lateral posterior portion of the pelvis, the sacrum, the coccyx, and the lower part of the spinal cord, having two bladders but one set of sexual organs, as well as one uterus and rectum. As to be expected, they were examined many times by doctors throughout their lives. It appears that they were educated by private tutors. It was also said that they spoke many languages. They were abducted when they were about ten years old, taken to England, and exhibited in a sideshow, but were later returned to their legal owner.

After the Civil War, they were freed. With money they had saved from their performances, they purchased the plantation on which they were born and built a ten-room house, where they lived between show engagements. During their lifetime, they performed throughout the world including performances before Queen Victoria

Mille-Christine on exhibit

and the Prince of Wales (Edward VII). Queen Victoria presented them with handsome matching broaches. Their stage appearances around the world offered more than a look at a freak of nature; they also sang and entertained, and never failed to impress their audience. They were sometimes billed as "The African Twins," "Carolina Twins," and "Carolina Nightingale." After 1900, they retired from show business and returned to their home in Whiteville. Mille died of tuberculosis on October 8, 1912, and Christine died seventeen hours later at the age of sixty-one. The twins were entertainers, performers, singers, linguists, deeply religious, and benevolent. Their marker is located on **US 74/76 northeast of Whiteville, Columbus County.**

WILMINGTON

Eight teachers from the American Missionary Association came to Wilmington, North Carolina, in 1865 to teach the newly freed Blacks. So many students wanted to go to school they eventually had to offer both day and night classes. A Mr. Williston, from Northhampton, Massachusetts, donated money to the association for the construction of a school building. They named the school Williston Academy. The school was subsequently named Wilmington Normal School and then New Hampshire Memorial Institute. In 1883, the name was changed again to **Gregory Normal Institute** in honor of Mr. James J.H. Gregory of Marblehead, Massachusetts, who gave money for the erection of a three-story brick building for the teachers' home, the enlargement of the school building, and the construction of a brick church. Over the years, Gregory Normal Institute graduates filled a large number of public school positions in Wilmington, greater New Hanover County, and adjoining states. Professor George A. Woodward, a former teacher at Gregory Normal Institute, said, "It pays to educate the Negro. Education may have spoiled quite a goodly number for washing dishes, sawing wood, or being bootblacks, but some of these people are now potent factors in the uplift and salvation of their race." The institution closed in 1921 after more than a half century of service to the city, county, and nation. The school marker is located on **US 17 Business (Third Street) at Nun Street in Wilmington, New Hanover County.**

James Francis Shober was born near Salem, North Carolina, which later became Winston-Salem, on August 23, 1853. He was probably educated by the Moravian community in that town. At any rate, he subsequently enrolled in Lincoln University in Pennsylvania in 1871 and graduated in 1875. Shober later attended and graduated from Howard University's Medical School in 1878. Dr. Shober decided to practice medicine in North Carolina and moved to Wilmington to open up a practice there in 1878, thus becoming the first Black to practice medicine in North Carolina with an M.D. At the time, he was the only Black physician in the largest city in the state, with a Black population of over ten thousand.

Dr. James Shober

Little is known about Dr. Shober while he was in Wilmington, except that he was successful, well-respected, married to Anna Maria Taylor, had two daughters, and was an Elder in the Chestnut Street Presbyterian Church. Dr. Shober died on January 1, 1889, at the young age of only thirty-six. Some attribute his early death to his strenuous workload. Dr. James Francis Shober was a pioneer in the practice of medicine among Blacks in Wilmington and in the state of North Carolina. He was a church Elder, a family man, and a good citizen. His marker is located on **US 17 Business (Market Street) at Eighth Street in Wilmington, New Hanover County.**

Although Blacks in Wilmington had been worshiping in a number of White Episcopal churches before 1869, after the autumn of that year, the congregation purchased a lot on the corner of Sixth and Mulberry (Grace) Streets and decided to have a church of their own. They adopted the name "St. Mark's Congregation." Reverend Charles Otis Brady, a Black deacon, led the effort to form the new church which would be built primarily by Blacks for Blacks. A sum of three thousand dollars was given by other Black and White citizens of Wilmington, as well as friends from the North, to help finance the building. According to the church records, "ground was broken for the new church on the sixth of March, 1871, and the cornerstone was laid on the twenty-third of the same month. The church was sufficiently completed, though far from being finished for the celebration of divine worship the ensuing December, when the congregation moved from St. Paul's to their own building." **St. Mark's** was consecrated on June 18, 1875, by the Right Reverend Thomas Atkinson, Bishop of the Diocese, thus becoming "the first Black Episcopal church in North Carolina." Since then, several additions helped improve the church's physical structure: bell tower, bell, vestry room, parish house, and rectory.

For over one hundred years, St. Mark's has stood at the corner of Grace and Sixth Streets, and services have been carried on without interruption. Thousands of children and adults have been baptized, confirmed, and have attended Sunday School and church services.

They have participated in many phases of church work, and given of their means, services, and gifts for the upbuilding of God's church. St. Mark's influence upon the spiritual and community life of Wilmington is intangible.

St. Mark's has offered a long and varied period of religious service to the Wilmington community and its environment. At crucial periods in its long existence, it has also played a significant part in giving other types of assistance to the community. The marker for St. Mark's Episcopal Church is located on **US 17 Business (Third Street) at Grace Street in Wilmington, New Hanover County.**

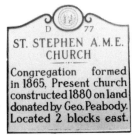

ST. STEPHEN A.M.E. CHURCH
Congregation formed in 1865. Present church constructed 1880 on land donated by Geo. Peabody. Located 2 blocks east.

The Black people of Wilmington, dissatisfied with their status in the White Methodist Church, decided in May 1865 to build their own church. Rev. W. H. Hunter, a Black Chaplain in the Union Army, spearheaded the drive, leading more than 640 Blacks to build the **St. Stephen African Methodist Episcopal (A.M.E.) Church**. Reverend James A. Hanby was appointed pastor of the new church by Bishop Daniel Payne of the African Methodist Episcopal Church Conference.

Succeeding Reverend Hanby were the Reverends Nichols, Seaton, Sluby, and Joseph Frye. Reverend Frye served the congregation from 1880 to 1885. During these years, construction of the present structure of St. Stephen A.M.E. Church began. Had it not been for the leadership of Reverend Frye and the deep devotion and dedication of the officers and members, most of whom were former slaves, this construction might have never been attempted. At a church meeting, it was decided to do away with the existing wooden building and erect a brick church. Nine stewards, nine trustees, and twenty-five class leaders were entrusted with the task of planning and executing the job. The land on which the present structure was erected was donated by Mr. George Peabody, a Boston philanthropist. The gift was channeled through the city of Wilmington, North Carolina.

Plans for the new structure were drawn by Lewis Hollinsworth, a brilliant, inspired architect, who was also one of the trustees. The bricks were made and furnished by Daniel Lee, another trustee, who owned and controlled a brickyard. Six master carpenters and a number of skilled bricklayers were members of the congregation. While officers and members dug out the basement, laid the foundation, and completed that area of the structure, the women of the church furnished dinners for the workers, and some even carried bricks in their aprons to assist the laborers with the construction. When the basement was completed, Reverend Frye marched his congregation into this area where services were subsequently held. The basement was completed by 1885. Through the years, a number of additions were made to the church. However, it still maintains most of its originality.

St. Stephen A.M.E. Church and its congregation have been a positive force in the community and have contributed greatly to the spiritual and secular well-being of the city, state, and nation. Its

St. Stephen A.M.E. Church

impact is intangible. For more than 125 years, St. Stephen has given spiritual assistance whenever it was needed. The church marker is located on **US 17 Business (Third Street) at Red Cross Street in Wilmington, New Hanover County.**

SOUTHERN PIEDMONT REGION

Fayetteville

FAYETTEVILLE

CHAS. W. CHESNUTT
1858 - 1932

Negro novelist and
short story writer,
teacher and lawyer.
Taught in a school
which stood here.

Charles W. Chesnutt's parents were born in Fayetteville, but because of the racial climate in the South, moved to Cleveland, Ohio. Their son, Charles Waddell Chesnutt, was born in Cleveland on June 20, 1858. After the Civil War, the Chesnutt family moved back to their native city and opened a grocery store. While in Fayetteville, Chesnutt attended Howard School; however, because he had to help support his eleven brothers and sisters, he did not finish high school. He managed to continue his education by studying on his own. He was only sixteen when he wrote "Lost in the Swamp." He was nineteen in 1877, when he became assistant to Principal Robert Harris of the new State Colored Normal School, later to become Fayetteville State University. Chesnutt was somewhat of a pupil-teacher because he continued to study on his own. When Harris died three years later in

1880, Chesnutt became principal of the Normal School. He became frustrated and disenchanted with the racial conditions in the South and moved back to Cleveland in 1883 after serving as a principal for only three years.

While in Cleveland, he continued to write as well as becoming a clerk-stenographer, court reporter, and attorney. His first love, however, was writing. While working full-time to support his family, he

wrote his first book, *The Conjure Woman,* in 1899. He subsequently wrote several other short stories, novels, biographies, and essays. Some contend that he was the first critically acclaimed Black writer. He died in Cleveland on November 15, 1932, at age seventy-four. Charles Waddell Chesnutt was an educator, college president, attorney, short-story writer, novelist, essayist, biographer, stenographer,

Charles Chesnutt

and an NAACP Spingarn Medalist. His marker is located on **Gillespie Street in Fayetteville, Cumberland County.**

HENRY EVANS

Free black cobbler & minister. Built first Methodist church in Fayetteville. Died 1810. Buried 2 blocks north.

Henry Evans was born free ca. 1760 in Virginia and was a shoemaker by trade. He later became a licensed minister in the Methodist church. It appears he was on his way to Charleston, South Carolina, in 1780, when he decided to stop in Fayetteville. While there, he noticed some free Blacks and slaves were without a preacher. He decided to stay in that city and preach to his race. At first, the local officials allowed him to preach. Later, however, they regarded Evans as an agitator, and forced him to move to the outskirts of town. They moved him from place to place. In time, when Whites realized that he was no threat to their lifestyle, he was allowed to preach again in Fayetteville. In fact, Whites saw a change in the manners and morals of his listeners.

Henry Evans was credited with building the first church, Black or White, in Fayetteville ca. 1796. It was said he built the church from rough boards he carried from a sawmill just across the creek. He lived in a room in back of the church, and did not own, but leased the land for seven years.

Reverend Evans became such a popular preacher even Whites in the surrounding areas attended his services, sitting in the seats reserved for them. Because Whites were attending the church in such large numbers, sheds had to be added on the sides of the church to accommodate the crowds. According to Bishop William Capers, Evans was "the father of the Methodist church, White and Black, in Fayetteville, and the best preacher of that time in that quarter."

Because of ill health in 1806, Reverend Evans had to give up his pastorship. In a unique will, dated December 9, 1809, Evans bequeathed the part of the building and lot used for church purposes to the Methodist Episcopal church. He did state, however, that his residence and the rest of the lot were to go to the church only after the death of his wife. Evans died September 17, 1810, at age fifty. His funeral was said to have been the largest ever held in that area, and was attended by both Blacks and Whites. He was buried under the chancel of the church he founded. Reverend Henry Evans was a cobbler, preacher, church founder, and a man of God. His marker is located on **Person Street at Cool Spring Street in Fayetteville, Cumberland County.**

In 1867, seven Black citizens, David Bryant, Nelson Carter, Matthew N. Leary, A. J. Chesnutt, Robert Simmons, George Grainer, and Thomas Lomax paid $140 for a lot on Gillespie Street in Fayetteville and converted themselves into a self-perpetuating Board of Trustees to maintain this property permanently as a site for the education of Black children in Fayetteville. General Oliver O. Howard erected a building on this site; thus, the institution became known as the "Howard School." Robert H. Harris was chosen as the principal and served until his demise in 1880, according to the school's history. In a legislative act of 1877, the North Carolina General Assembly provided for the establishment of a Normal School for the education of Black teachers. Because of the small amount of the appropriation, the assembly felt that the money could be used more effectively if given to an existing school. Several

Robert Harris

areas of the state competed to have this state-supported school, but the legislature chose the Howard School as the most promising because of its success record during the previous ten years. It was designated a teacher training institution and its name was changed to the State Colored Normal School. Charles Waddell Chesnutt, formerly assistant to Principal Harris, became the second principal of the institution in 1880.

In 1883, Principal Chesnutt resigned and Dr. Ezekiel Ezra Smith was selected to fill the vacancy. George Williams was chosen to guide the school between 1888-1895. Reverend L. E. Fairley became acting principal of State Normal School between 1898-1899. When Dr. Smith retired in 1933 as president of the State Normal School, the institution had moved to its present location. In 1929, all high school work was discontinued at the Normal School. In May of 1937, the State Board of Education authorized the extension of study to four years with authority to grant the bachelor of science degree in elementary education.   In 1939, the name of the institution was changed to Fayetteville State Teachers College and was under the leadership of Dr. James Ward Seabrook, who served as president from 1933 until his retirement in 1956.   In 1969, the institution was given the name **Fayetteville State University** and became a regional university.   On October 30, 1971, Fayetteville State University became a constituent of The University of North Carolina, effective July 1, 1972. The marker for the institution is located on **NC 210 in Fayetteville, Cumberland County.**

TRIANGLE REGION

Durham
Raleigh

DURHAM

On July 5, 1910, James E. Shepard chartered a private institution known as the National Religious Training School and Chautaugua, on Fayetteville Street in Durham, North Carolina. B. N. Duke, the tobacco magnate, and the Durham Merchants Association purchased the land for Shepard. By the end of 1910, Shepard had raised about seven thousand dollars from friends and supporters from both the North and the South. With that money, he was able to construct six buildings, including a home for the president. One of Shepard's main reasons for starting the school was the training of ministers. He believed the leaders of his people would come from this school. He had as the school's motto "Truth and Service." In 1915, the school was reorganized and the name changed to the National Training School. In 1923, the state of North Carolina began financially supporting the institution, and the school now became known as the Durham State Normal School. In 1925, there was another reorganization and another name change, to the North Carolina College for

Negroes. This school was the first state-supported liberal arts college for Blacks in the United States. The year Dr. Shepard died, 1947, the school was called North Carolina College at Durham. In 1969, the institution's name was changed to **North Carolina Central University** (NCCU). In 1972, NCCU became a constituent institution of The University of North Carolina. Over the years, NCCU has had a School of Law, School of Library and Science, and School of Nursing. It has graduated thousands of students who have made significant contributions to many fields of endeavor. The university's marker is located on **NC 55 (Alston Avenue) at Lawson Street in Durham, Durham County.**

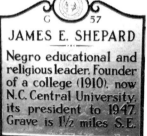

James Edward Shepard was born in Raleigh, North Carolina, on November 3, 1875. He attended Shaw University and graduated in 1894 with a degree in pharmacy. He later studied theology between 1894 and 1898. In 1898, he worked in Washington, D.C., in former Congressman, Henry P. Cheatham's office as Comparer of Deeds. A year later, he returned to North Carolina. During that year, he was one of the founders of the North Carolina Mutual and Provident Association, later to become North Carolina Mutual Life Insurance Company. In the same year, he became Deputy Collector of Internal Revenue for the United States government. It was said that he was the first and only Black to serve in that position in North Carolina during his time. He held that position until 1905. Between 1905 and 1909, Dr. Shepard served as Field Superintendent of the International Sunday School Association, working primarily among Blacks. In 1910, he founded the National Religious Training School and Chautauqua in Durham, North Carolina (later North Carolina

James Shepard

College at Durham and now North Carolina Central University). Shepard served as president of that institution until his death in 1947, at age seventy-two. James Edward Shepard was a registered pharmacist, educator, politician, churchman, businessman, founder of a college, ordained minister, and leader. His marker is located on **NC 75 (Hope Valley Road) at University Drive in Durham, Durham County.**

RALEIGH

John Chavis, born ca. 1763 in Virginia, was probably an indentured servant. He served about three years in the Revolutionary Army between 1778 and 1781. It appears that he was tutored by William Willie during the time he spent as an indentured servant. Some records indicate Chavis attended the Presbyterian Washington Academy, later to be renamed Washington and Lee University. Chavis later attended Princeton University where he received private instructions from Dr. John Witherspoon, president of Princeton. Some believe Chavis was the most educated Black of his time in the nation.

In 1800, Chavis received a license to preach from the Presbyterian Church of Lexington, Virginia. Between 1801 and 1807, he did missionary work among slaves and free Blacks in Maryland, Virginia, and North Carolina. Chavis subsequently settled in Raleigh, North Carolina and preached to both Blacks and Whites. While in Raleigh, Chavis also opened a school and taught both Black and White students. A number of his White students were from prominent families. Several of his former students went on to become governor, attorneys, politicians, and judges. Because of the Nat Turner rebellion in 1831,

Blacks were no longer permitted to preach, forcing Chavis into retirement. A year before his death in 1837, he published an essay entitled *Chavis' Letter Upon the Doctrine of the Atonement of Christ*. He died June 15, 1838, at about age seventy. John Chavis was a preacher, teacher, scholar, essayist, Federalist, and friend of the prominent and wealthy. His marker is located on **East Street at Worth Street in Raleigh, Wake County.**

James Henry Harris was born a slave in 1832 in Granville County, North Carolina. He acquired his freedom in 1848 when he learned the carpentry trade, probably self-taught. In 1860, he attended Oberlin College in Ohio. Harris traveled to Canada, Liberia, and Sierra Leone in 1862. In 1863, he was commissioned by Governor Levi Morton of Indiana to help raise the Twenty-Eighth Regiment of the United States Colored Troops. Two years later, he came back to Raleigh and taught school for the New England Freedman's Aid Society. In 1865, he attended the North Carolina Freedman's Convention; a year later, he was elected president of the convention. In 1868, Harris was a delegate to the North Carolina Constitutional Convention. During the same year, he was appointed as the first Black Alderman for the city of Raleigh. Later in 1868, Harris was elected to the North Carolina House of Representatives. He served three terms. Harris also served one term as a state senator.

James H. Harris participated in a number of other political activities and appointments during his lifetime. He was a Deputy Tax Collector, delegate to several Republican National Conventions, president of the National Convention of Colored Men, and vice-president of the National Black Convention.

As a politician, Harris advocated moderation on racial matters and reconciliation with Whites. He did, however, emphasize the need for education for Blacks and an end to legal and racial discrimination. Harris also had concern for the Black deaf, dumb, and blind. He was instrumental in helping erect an institution for them in Raleigh where he served on the first trustee board. Besides being called "the finest statesman of his color in North Carolina," Harris was also editor and publisher of The North Carolina Republican in the 1880s. The newspaper's goal was to work "in behalf of the Republican Party and the advancement of the Negro." He died May 31, 1891 at age fifty-nine. James Henry Harris was a politician, educator, newspaperman, editor, state representative, state senator, benefactor, churchman and leader of his people. His marker is located on **Person Street at Davie Street in Raleigh, Wake County.**

Edward Austin Johnson was born a slave on November 23, 1860 to Columbus and Eliza Johnson, in Wake County. After slavery, he attended Washington School in Raleigh and graduated from Atlanta University in 1883. In 1885, he returned to Raleigh and became principal and teacher at the Washington School. In 1891, he published *A School History of the Negro Race in America*. This work was the first textbook by a Black author to be approved by the North Carolina State Board of Education to be used in the classroom. Johnson wrote four other books, including *History of the Negro Soldier in the Spanish-American War, Light Ahead for the Negro*, and *Negro Almanac and Statistics*. He also wrote several pamphlets and articles.

In 1891, he graduated from Shaw University Law School and two years later taught law there, becoming dean. Johnson was elected from the Fourth Ward as a member of Raleigh's Board of Aldermen.

He served one term. Between 1899 and 1907, he was an assistant in the United States District Attorney's office for eastern North Carolina.

Because of racial tension and reportedly, lack of sufficient Black clientele, Johnson left North Carolina and moved to New York City in 1907. He opened a law office in Harlem. In 1910, he was elected to

the New York State Assembly, thus becoming the first Black member of the New York Legislature. He only served a term and was defeated for re-election, mainly due to redistricting of his area. Johnson was never again elected to a political office although, over the years, he did serve as a Republican district chairman and was a delegate to three Republican national conventions.

Edward Johnson

Blinded from cataracts during the latter part of his life, Mr. Johnson stipulated in his will that half of the income from his sizable estate be used to aid Black blind people in Raleigh and Wake County, and that the other half go to the First Congregational Church in Raleigh. The church was instructed to use a portion of its receipts for expenses and the remainder for scholarship purposes. Johnson died July 24, 1944, at age eighty-three. Edward Austin Johnson was an educator, historian, author, attorney, politician, and benefactor. His marker is located on **West Street at Lenoir Street in Raleigh, Wake County.**

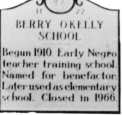

BERRY O'KELLY
SCHOOL

Begun 1910. Early Negro
teacher training school.
Named for benefactor.
Later used as elementary
school. Closed in 1966.

Berry O'Kelly School was the brain child of its benefactor, Berry O'Kelly, who was born in Wake County in 1860. While serving as chairman of the local school committee, in 1914, he succeeded in consolidating three rural Black schools in Wake County into the Berry O'Kelly Training School in the section of Raleigh known as Method. He served as chairman of the school committee while H. L. Trigg was its principal. This was a four-year high school. It had eight teachers and was one of only three such schools to be accredited by the state of North Carolina. The students were required to complete fifteen units in order to graduate, including science, mathematics, history, and language. Vocational agriculture, food, clothing, and economics were also taught. The school was later used as an elementary school and closed in 1966, after serving the Black community for over fifty years.

Besides being an educator, Berry O'Kelly was also a successful businessman. He owned a general store, realty company, and shoe company. He was also chairman of a life insurance company and vice-president of the Raleigh branch of the Mechanics and Farmers Bank of Durham. He died in 1931 at age seventy-one. The school's marker is located on **Method Road in Raleigh, Wake County.**

On December 1, 1865, Henry Martin Tupper, a White man from Monson, Massachusetts, assembled a class of Blacks in a room of the Old Guion Hotel, located in the Capitol Square area of Raleigh, North Carolina. Tupper's announced purpose for the class was to provide instruction in the Bible in order that these freedmen might become leaders and establish churches, conventions, and associations to carry on the work of the Baptist church. As this class grew in size, it formed the basis for the organization of a school, the Raleigh Institute, which became a part of the church-school complex erected in 1866 out of funds provided by the New England Freedman's Aid Society and Tupper's savings from his Civil War service. In 1870, the school was relocated to the Daniel Barringer estate facing East South Street, which had been purchased for thirteen thousand dollars. The purchase was made possible through Elijah Shaw, a woolen goods manufacturer of Wales, Massachusetts, who contributed five thousand dollars, the Freedman's Bureau, which gave four thousand dollars, and solicitations made by Tupper himself in the amount of four thousand dollars. The school erected on this site became known as Shaw Collegiate Institute.

In 1875, it was incorporated as **The Shaw University**, named for its principal benefactor, Elijah Shaw. The character of the school indicates its establishment without respect to race, creed, or sex. It has been church-related and supported by the Baptists as well as being coeducational from its inception. The first college class was graduated in 1878. In 1881, the university established the Leonard Medical School, the first four-year medical school in the nation. This was followed by the establishment of a law school in 1886 and a pharmacy school in 1891. In 1918, as a result of inadequate financial resources, the schools of medicine, law, and pharmacy were closed.

The major emphases of the university were expressed through the School of Theology and the College of Arts and Sciences. While modifications have brought about the deletion of the professional schools on one hand, and the separation of the Divinity School on the other, the original purpose of training teachers remains the expressed goal of the institution. Existing goals of the university, however, embrace more than the training of teachers, for the institution trains large numbers of students for a variety of fields. Through the decades the university has continued to adjust its goals and objectives within the general framework of its motto, "Pro Christo et Humanitate." Shaw University's graduates have gone on to become teachers, ministers, doctors, lawyers, pharmacists, and many other professions. The university marker is located on **South Street in Raleigh, Wake County.**

ST. AUGUSTINE'S
COLLEGE
Founded in 1867 by the
Episcopal Church as a
normal school for freed-
men. Since 1928 a four-
year college. 4 blocks N.

St. Augustine's College was founded in 1867 by the Episcopal Church as a school for the instruction of Black people in the South. Twenty-five thousand dollars had been secured from a bequest as a capital fund for the new school, and the federal Freedman's Bureau had given $6,243 for the construction of buildings. Reverend Jacob Brinton Smith resigned his office as secretary and general agent of the Freedman's Commission in November of 1867 to become the school's first principal. The Raleigh *Tri-Weekly Standard* carried an advertisement of the school's opening set for January 13, 1868, and instruction began that day with four pupils. The school was first located in the "Howard School House" on the site of the later Confederate Soldiers' Home. The main emphasis of the school was the training of teachers. A second emphasis was the training of students to be admitted to the Episcopal priesthood.

In 1896, St. Agnes Hospital was built on St. Augustine's campus, with a mostly White medical staff. This hospital was closed in 1961. In 1896, the first Benson Library was also begun. Although St. Augustine's College began as a normal school, in 1928, the state of North Carolina accredited it as a four-year college. Over its more than 120 year history, St. Augustine's College has graduated students that have become teachers, priests, ministers, doctors, nurses, community leaders, college presidents, writers, and attorneys. The college marker is located on **Edenton Street at Tarboro Road in Raleigh, Wake County.**

James Hunter Young was born in Henderson, North Carolina, on October 26, 1858. He attended school in Henderson and graduated from Shaw University in 1877. Young held a number of positions after graduating from college: Collector of Internal Revenue for the Fourth District in Raleigh, Chief Clerk in the Office of Register of Deeds in Wake County, and Special Inspector of Customs. In 1880, he served as a delegate to the State Republican Convention. Between 1892 and 1898, he was owner and editor of the weekly Raleigh Gazette. In 1892, he was elected by Wake County, a county which had a White population of fifty-three percent, to the North Carolina House of Representatives. Young was a prominent Black in the state legislature during the Fusion period, during which he received many unfriendly comments from the Democratic press. The Fusion period (1895-1901) was the time when the People's party and the Republican party merged and gained power over the Democratic party, after the Democrats had dominated politics. The Democrats restored dominance in 1901.

Young served two terms between 1894 and 1896. While in the General Assembly, he was appointed to a number of important committees: Judiciary, Privileges and Election, Finance, Special Election Law, Institutions for the Blind, Education, Printing, and Colonial Records. He was chairman of the committee to fill the vacancies of the Board of Trustees at the state-supported, Black A&M College (now A&T State University in Greensboro). Young also served on county government committees as well as on committees to oversee the insane asylums. While in the General Assembly, he proposed and was responsible for the passage of a number of bills. Young's proposals resulted in increased funding for the deaf, dumb, and blind institutions and for A&M College, as well as for the paving of the streets around Capitol Square. He also proposed that the seven Black state normal schools receive direct state aid.

In 1897, Young was appointed Chief Fertilizer Inspector for the state of North Carolina. Also during that year, he was appointed to the Board of Directors for the Deaf, Dumb, and Blind Institutions. In 1898, James H. Young was made a colonel of the Black regiment which volunteered for the Spanish-American War. Colonel Young was the

James Young

organizer and commanding officer of the Third North Carolina Infantry. The regiment trained in North Carolina, Georgia, and Tennessee. While in Tennessee, Young was promoted to Brigadier General. The regiment, however, was never ordered to Cuba to fight in the war. James Hunter Young died in 1921 at age sixty-one. He was a politician, state legislator, newspaperman, editor, promoter of education, businessman, and fraternal leader. His marker is located on **Person Street at Lenoir Street in Raleigh, Wake County.**

As this book went to press, another highway marker was erected at the Raleigh City Cemetery honoring Afro-Americans buried there, including educator, Anna Cooper.

TRIAD REGION

Greensboro
Sedalia
Winston-Salem

GREENSBORO

Bennett College was founded in 1873 as a coeducational institution. Its first sessions were held in the basement of the St. Matthews Methodist Episcopal Church in Greensboro, North Carolina. The college was the inspiration of newly emancipated slaves, who bought the land on which the college now stands. As a result of the appeal by the founders for assistance, the Freedmen's Aid, and Southern Education Society of the Methodist Episcopal Church assumed responsibility for the support of the school. Lyman Bennett gave the first ten thousand dollars for the erection of a building large enough to house the classrooms and a dormitory. The institution was named Bennett Seminary to honor the memory of their benefactor, and the first building was named Bennett Hall.

Early in this century, the Woman's Home Missionary Society decided to build a college for the education of Black women. The Board of Education of the Methodist Church offered the site of Bennett College for this project, proposing that the Missionary

172

Society and the Board of Education would jointly operate the college. Under these two agencies Bennett College became one of the two senior colleges for Black women in the South.

Since the reorganization of the institution as a college for women, it has achieved high accreditation. In 1930, on the graduation of its first young women with the bachelor of arts degree, the North Carolina State Department of Education granted the college the "A" rating. This same rating was granted in 1935 by the Southern Association of Colleges and Secondary Schools. In 1957, Bennett was one of the first Black colleges to be admitted into full membership in the Southern Association of Colleges and Secondary Schools. Over its more than 110 year history, Bennett College's graduates have assumed positions of leadership as preachers, teachers, and homemakers as well as leaders in other professions. The college's marker is located on **US 421 (East Market Street) at Dudley Street in Greensboro, Guilford County.**

IMMANUEL COLLEGE
Lutheran. Founded 1903, and moved here in 1905; prepared black students for work in theology & education. Closed 1961.

Immanuel Lutheran College was founded in 1903 in Concord, North Carolina and moved to Greensboro in 1905. It was owned, operated, and supported by the Lutheran Synodical Conference of North Carolina. Reverend Niels Bakke, a White Lutheran pastor, was the first president of the college and served from 1903 through 1911. The college was established as a missionary institution which had the double purpose of preparing young men and women as ministers and teachers for the churches and schools in the Lutheran Black Mission, and of offering Black youths an opportunity to receive a higher education under distinctive Lutheran Christian influences and principles. The college also encouraged and stimulated educational growth and development in the classroom as well as in everyday life.

The curriculum was broad and varied and fitted the needs of most students seeking general academic training in the high school or junior college area.

Thousands of Black students attended and graduated from Immanuel Lutheran College over its nearly sixty year history. Some of its former students include Dr. James Cheek, former president of Howard University, Actor Greg Morris of "Mission Impossible," and James Wright, former Director of Human Rights for the city of Greensboro, North Carolina. The school closed in 1961 when Lutheran Church officials decided that, because of the changing educational integration policy of society, it was not necessary to have a school exclusively for Black students. There is a marker for the institution located on **US 70/421 (East Market Street) at Benbow Road in Greensboro, Guilford County.**

North Carolina Agricultural and Technical State University was established as the A. and M. College for the "Colored Race" by an act of the General Assembly of North Carolina, ratified March 9, 1891. The college actually began operation during the school year of 1890-1891, before passage of the state law creating it. This curious circumstance arose out of the fact that the Morrill Act, passed by congress in 1890, earmarked the proportionate funds to be allocated in biracial school systems. The A. and M. College for the White Race was established by the state legislature in 1889 and was ready to receive its share of funds provided by the Morrill Act in the fall of 1890. Before the college could receive these funds, however, it was necessary to make provisions for Colored students. Accordingly, the Board of Trustees of A. and M. College in Raleigh was empowered to make temporary arrangements for these students. A plan was worked out in Raleigh whereby A. and M. College would operate as an annex to Shaw University during the years 1890-1891, 1891-1892, and 1892-1893, according to A. & T.'s history.

The law of 1891 also provided that the Board of Trustees would decide where to locate the college, based on the proposals received  from the interested cities and towns in the state. A group of citizens in the city of Greensboro donated fourteen acres of land for a site and eleven thousand dollars to aid in constructing the buildings. This amount was supplemented by an appropriation of $2,500 from the General Assembly. The first building was completed in 1893, and the college opened in Greensboro during the fall of that year, as states

John Crosby

the school's records. Dr. John Crosby served as its first president. He served from 1892 to 1896.

In 1915, the name of the institution was changed to The Agricultural and Technical College of North Carolina by an act of the state legislature. The General Assembly of North Carolina voted to elevate the college to the status of a regional university effective July 1, 1967. On October 30, 1971, North Carolina Agricultural and Technical State University became a constituent institution of The University of North Carolina, effective July 1, 1972. The marker for the school is located on **US 220 (Wendover Avenue) in Greensboro, Guilford County.**

On February 1, 1960, four young Black students from North Carolina A&T State College sat down in a previously reserved "for White only" section of an F. W. Woolworth Store lunch counter in Greensboro and refused to leave until they were served. They were not served.

These students started a sit-in movement in Greensboro that would have world-wide repercussions and affect millions of people. William H. Chafe, in his book, *Civilities and Civil Rights*, argued: "The Greensboro sit-ins inaugurated the passive resistance phase of the civil rights revolution, shaping the history of a decade." The marker is located on **Elm Street at Friendly Avenue, Guilford** County.

Woolworth Store, Greensboro

SEDALIA

PALMER MEMORIAL
INSTITUTE
Preparatory school for
blacks founded 1902 by
Charlotte Hawkins Brown.
Named for Alice Freeman
Palmer. Closed in 1971.
Now state historic site.

Charlotte Hawkins was born in Henderson, North Carolina in 1883. During her childhood, her family moved to Cambridge, Massachusetts. While in Cambridge, Miss Hawkins attended Cambridge English High School and Salem State Normal School.

While she was a student at Salem, the American Missionary Association offered her a teaching position in North Carolina. Dissatisfied with the lack of educational opportunities for Blacks in the South, Hawkins accepted. She returned to North Carolina in 1901 to teach rural Black children in Bethany Congregational Church in

Charlotte Brown

Sedalia, Guilford County. The school closed after one term, but young Hawkins decided to remain in the community and establish her own school. She was only eighteen years old at the time. In 1902, after vigorously raising money in the New England area, Charlotte Hawkins founded **Palmer Institute** in Sedalia, a day and boarding school for Blacks. Established in a converted blacksmith's shop, the school was named in honor of Alice Freeman Palmer, Charlotte's friend and chief benefactor. Mrs. Palmer was also the first woman president of Wellesley College in Massachusetts. Under the leadership of Charlotte

Hawkins Brown, Palmer Memorial Institute became a nationally recognized and respected preparatory school for Blacks.

In its early years, Palmer's curriculum emphasized manual training and industrial education for rural living. Brown expanded the school to over 350 acres of land, including a sizable farm. As the thirties came to a close, both the school's academic importance and its emphasis on cultural education increased. During Dr. Brown's tenure as president of Palmer Memorial, over one thousand students graduated. Many went on to become national leaders. Dr. Brown died in 1961. In 1971, Palmer Memorial Institute closed its doors. The institute marker is located on **US 70 in Sedalia, Guilford County.**

WINSTON-SALEM

In 1890, Simon Green Atkins was principal of the Depot School in Winston, North Carolina (now Winston-Salem). He later founded a school for Blacks in the Columbian Heights area of the city. He and his family were the first settlers in that area. Atkins called the school Slater Industrial Academy. It began classes on September 28, 1892 in a one-room, frame structure with twenty-five students and one teacher. The school was named after John F. Slater, a White philanthropist who had set up a foundation in New York and donated money for the academy. The school was private. In 1895, it was recognized by the state of North Carolina. In 1897, the state gave it a charter and called it the State Normal School at Winston. Later it was called the Slater Industrial and State Normal School. It was also called the Slater State Normal School.

Simon Atkins

Until 1922, the school was little more than a two-year college. In 1925, the General Assembly of North Carolina granted the institution a new charter under the name of Winston-Salem Teachers College (WSTC) and empowered it to confer appropriate degrees. Thus, WSTC became the first Black institution in the United States to grant degrees for teaching in the elementary grades. In 1963, the name was changed once again to Winston-Salem State College. The school was given university status by the state in 1969 and named **Winston-Salem State University (WSSU)**. In 1972, WSSU became a constituent of The University of North Carolina. Over its nearly one hundred year history, Winston-Salem State University has lived up to its motto, "Enter to Learn, Depart to Serve," and has produced graduates who have become teachers, doctors, lawyers, politicians, college presidents, athletes, coaches, professionals, and community leaders. The institution's marker is located on **US 311 (Martin Luther King, Jr. Boulevard) in Winston-Salem, Forsyth County.**

NORTHERN PIEDMONT REGION

Blanch   Milton

Franklinton   Oxford

Haw River   Warrenton

BLANCH

BRIGHT LEAF TOBACCO
In 1850s on a farm in this area Abisha Slade perfected a process for curing yellow tobacco. His slave Stephen discovered process in 1839.

In her book, *The Bright Tobacco Industry, 1860-1929*, Miss Nannie May Tilley credited Stephen Slade, a slave of Abisha Slade, with the discovery of the process for curing yellow tobacco. It seems Stephen Slade was born in 1821 and worked as foreman and blacksmith on Abisha Slade's farm in Caswell County. In 1839, when Stephen was only eighteen years old, he "accidentally" discovered the process. During that year, Stephen was watching a barn of curing tobacco and fell asleep. When he woke up, he saw that the fire was almost out. He immediately went to a nearby charcoal pit and took some charred butts of logs, placing them on the dying fire. This produced the brightest yellow tobacco ever seen in that area. Years later, several newspapers, such as Progressive Farmer, April 14, 1886, gave Stephen's account of what happened on that rainy night in 1839. Stephen asserted in part, "...to tell the truth about it, 'twas an accident. I commenced to cure it and it commenced to git yallow. It kep' on yallowin' and kep' on yallowin' and kep' on yallowin' twell it got clar up...It looked so purty. I kept making it yallow and when it was cured it was 'musement for folks to come and see it." This discovery by Stephen Slade, a slave, revolutionized tobacco curing in North Carolina. Over the years after the discovery, Abisha Slade and his family perfected the process for curing yellow tobacco. This highway marker is located on **NC 64, on Blanch Road in Blanch, Caswell County.**

FRANKLINTON

E 62

MOSES A. HOPKINS

U.S. Minister to Liberia. 1885-1886. Negro clergyman. Founder & principal of Albion Academy which stood 2 blocks E.

Moses Aaron Hopkins was born a slave on December 25, 1846, in Montgomery County, Virginia. During the Civil War, he was a cook for the Union Army, and he did not learn to read until about 1866, when he was twenty years old. Hopkins subsequently attended Avery College in Pennsylvania and Lincoln University in the same state, where he graduated at the head of his class in 1874. Not content with his education, he studied for the ministry at Auburn Seminary in New York and was reported to have been the first Black to graduate from that institution; he graduated in 1877. Hopkins was ordained in the ministry the same year and moved to Franklinton, North Carolina, to become pastor of a Presbyterian church. He supposedly founded other Presbyterian churches in Franklinton, Henderson, and Rocky Ford. While in Franklinton, he founded Albion Academy as a boarding school and operated it for Black youths for about eight years. He may have also been the editor of the *Gazette* while he was in Franklinton.

In 1885, Mr. Hopkins was appointed United States Minister Resident and Consul General to Liberia. He served in this capacity until his death. He died in Monrovia, Liberia, on August 7, 1886, at age forty. Moses Aaron Hopkins was a minister, educator, editor, and diplomat. His marker is located on **US lA (Main Street) in Franklinton, Franklin County.**

HAW RIVER

The **Dr. Charles R. Drew Memorial** marker is located in Alamance County. It has been written again and again that Dr. Drew died because he was refused medical treatment in a White-only hospital in Alamance County after he was injured in a car accident close-by. County residents, including his daughter, put to rest once and for all that rumor and erected a marker near the site of the accident. The state of North Carolina, which will only pay for markers for native North Carolinians, did not fund the memorial since Dr. Drew was not a native of the state. Therefore, private and matching donations were collected by Ms. Gilberta Mitchell, who came up with the proposal for the marker.

Dr. Charles R. Drew was born in Washington, DC in 1904. He graduated from Amherst College in 1926 and from McGill University Medical School in 1933. Dr. Drew also received the Doctor of Medical Science degree from Columbia University's College of Physicians and Surgeons in 1940. While working in New York, he discovered blood plasma, which could be kept for months. This discovery saved thousands of soldiers' lives during World War II. In 1941, Dr. Drew was appointed Director of the American Red Cross project to bank the blood of one hundred thousand donors. He died in Alamance County on April 1, 1950, from injuries sustained in a car accident. Part of US 49 North highway is named the Dr. Charles R. Drew Memorial Highway. His memorial marker is located **off of US I-85 about two miles north of Haw River on US 49 North.**

MILTON

G 93
THOMAS DAY
Ca. 1801-1861
Free black cabinetmaker in Milton. 1824-1861. Home and shop located here in the old Union Tavern. 1848-1858.

Thomas Day was born in Halifax County, Virginia ca. 1801. Some writers contend that at an early age (perhaps ten years old) a wealthy lady sent him to cabinetmaking school in Boston and Washington after having seen him make a stool. Little else is known about his youth. It seems that he opened a furniture shop in his home county in 1818. He subsequently moved to Milton, North Carolina, in 1823, and shortly thereafter opened a shop. In 1830, Day married Acquilla Wilson, a free Black woman from Halifax County, Virginia. When North Carolina's 1827 immigration law, however, prevented her from coming into the state, the White citizens of Milton petitioned the North Carolina General Assembly for a waiver so that Mrs. Day could live in the state without fines or penalties. The state granted the citizens' request, and she was allowed to live in Milton with her husband.

From 1827 to the 1850s, Day purchased a number of business holdings in Milton. In 1827, he purchased property for his shop, and in 1834, he acquired stock in a state bank. In 1848, Thomas Day purchased Union Tavern, at one time the largest and finest tavern in the area. He did not, however, run it as a tavern. Instead, he converted it into a shop and his residence. Day was more than a cabinetmaker. He also made fine furniture, bedsteads, chairs, tables, French sofas, benches, pews, etc. At one time, he employed twelve workers in his shop. Some writers contend that he controlled about "one-fourth of the investment by all carpenters and builders in the state." Thomas Day's furniture was purchased by some of the leading White families in the state and South.

Thomas Day had three children, Mary Ann, Devereux, and Thomas, Jr. He wanted a good education for them; therefore, he sent them to Wilbraham Academy in Massachusetts. Day died in Milton in 1861 at age sixty. Thomas Day was a cabinetmaker, craftsman, carpenter, contractor, businessman, property owner, churchman, and respected citizen. His marker is located on **NC 62/57 (Broad Street) in Milton, Caswell County.**

OXFORD

Henry Plummer Cheatham was born a slave on December 27, 1857 in Henderson, North Carolina. Little is known of his childhood except that he may have had a tutor. At any rate, he attended Shaw University and graduated in 1883 with a law degree. Instead of practicing law, he became teacher and principal of a school in Plymouth, North Carolina. Between 1884 and 1888, Cheatham was elected Register of Deeds in Vance County. In 1888, he was elected to the United States Congress from the Second Congressional District. In 1890, he was re-elected and served until 1893, when he was defeated for a third term. While in Congress, he sponsored and supported a number of bills: Aid-to-Education, Silver Purchase Act, and government protection of depositors of the Freedman's Bank. Unfortunately, none of his bills were enacted. Although he was elected from the so-called "Black Second District," he supported legislation that would benefit both Blacks and Whites. He was relatively successful in obtaining federal appointments for his constituents and friends. He even offered Joseph Charles Price, founder of Livingstone College, a federal appointment, but Price rejected it. Cheatham was respected by both his supporters and political opponents, Black and White. He had the confidence of the people of both races. Mr. Cheatham was described "as a man of good grace and intellectual stature."

Between 1897 and 1901, he was appointed by President William McKinley as Register of Deeds in Washington, DC. After Cheatham retired from his position in Washington, he returned to North Carolina. In 1907, he took over the management of the Colored Orphan Asylum at Oxford. Perhaps his greatest accomplishment was the upgrading of the asylum. He was superintendent of it for more than twenty-seven years. He funded the institution with his own money as well as funds solicited from wealthy Whites, such as Ben-

Henry Cheatham

jamin N. Duke. When Cheatham left the asylum, it included several acres of farmland, brick buildings, housing, school facilities, brickyard, and sawmill. He died November 29, 1935, at age seventy-eight. Henry Plummer Cheatham was a politician, educator, orator, intellect, benefactor, and leader of his race. His marker is located on **NC 96 (Linden Avenue) at Eighth Street in Oxford, Granville County.**

In 1883, the Colored Orphanage Association met in Henderson, North Carolina and founded the Colored Orphanage of North Carolina. In October of that year, the association purchased a farm of twenty-three acres located one and one-half miles from Oxford on the Raleigh Road. The Orphanage was named the "Grant Colored Asylum." In 1887, the name was changed again to "The Colored Orphanage Asylum of North Carolina" and was incorporated as a nondenominational institution to receive children deprived of their parents and means of support. Its goal was to train the orphans along religious, moral, and industrial lines to enable them to become useful, law-abiding citizens. The orphanage accepted children from throughout the United States. The members of the first Board of Directors were the Reverends Dr. Augustus Shepard, Joshua Perry, W. A. Patillo, Isaac Alston, and J. W. Levy, as well as M. F. Thornton, H. E. Long, Henry Hester, and former United States Congressman Henry P. Cheatham. Various members of the Board served as superintendent of the orphanage at one time or another.

Benefactors from religious, philanthropic, and civic organizations throughout the states supported the orphanage. The state of North Carolina also gave annual appropriations. Up until 1927, only Blacks served on the Board of Trustees. In 1927, the name was changed to "The Colored Orphanage of North Carolina" and the governor of North Carolina was authorized to appoint five White men to the Board of Directors.

Over the years, the orphanage added more buildings and land until it reached the size of four hundred acres. The young people have been taught a number of trades: brickmaking, shoe repair, farming, dairying, general repair, lawn care, serving, cooking, and general housekeeping. In 1965, the name of the orphanage was once again changed to **The Central Orphanage of North Carolina**. In August 1986, the facility became known as the Central Children's

Home of North Carolina, Inc. Its marker is located on **NC 96 in Oxford, Granville County.**

WARRENTON

John Adams Hyman was born a slave on July 23, 1840, near Warrenton in Warren County. He was sold and sent to Alabama and stayed there until about 1865. In 1865, he returned to Warrenton a free man. It appeared that he was educated rudimentarily by a Warrenton jeweler. During 1866, Hyman was a delegate to the second Freedman's Convention. In 1867, he was a delegate to the first Republican State Convention. A year later, he was a delegate to the North Carolina Constitutional Convention in Raleigh. In 1868, he was elected as a State Senator from Warren County and served until 1874. He supported civil rights bills during his tenure. While in the State Senate, Hyman was involved in a number of questionable deals such as payoffs, and allegedly accepted money from lobbyists and demanded money from a congressional candidate in return for his support.

He ran for a United States Congressional seat in 1872, but was defeated. In 1874, however, he was elected to Congress, thus becoming the first Black Congressman from North Carolina. He served from March 4, 1875 through March 3, 1877. While in Congress, he supported all legislation concerning civil rights and suffrage rights for Blacks. Hyman was not elected to Congress for a second term because he did not receive his party's endorsement, did not have enough Black support, and had past allegations of fraud during his time in the State Senate.

Hyman returned to private life and resumed agricultural pursuits. He became Special Deputy of Internal Revenue for the Fourth District of North Carolina from July 1, 1877 to June 1, 1878. Around 1880, he left Warrenton and moved to Washington, D. C. While in the nation's capital, he found employment as an assistant mail clerk with the

John Hyman

United States Post Office. He held that position for nine years. Hyman later worked for the United States Agriculture Department. He died of a stroke on September 14, 1891, at age fifty-one. John Adams Hyman was a politician, state senator, congressman, businessman, and federal employee. His marker is located on **US 401 (South Main Street) at Franklin Street in Warrenton, Warren County.**

METROLINA REGION

Concord
Lincolnton
Salisbury

CONCORD

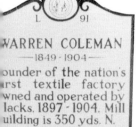

WARREN COLEMAN
—1849-1904—
ounder of the nation's
rst textile factory
wned and operated by
lacks. 1897-1904. Mill
uilding is 350 yds. N.

Warren Clay Coleman was born a slave on March 28, 1849, in Concord, North Carolina. During slavery, he learned the shoemaker trade. He was also educated in his youth by a White planter-lawyer. After slavery, he left North Carolina and moved to Alabama in search of better economic opportunities. In 1871, Coleman returned to Concord and became a merchant. He attended Howard University from 1873 to 1874. He subsequently returned to Concord and opened up a barber shop and general store. In a matter of years, he acquired substantial property in Cabarrus County and became one of the wealthiest men in the area.

Warren C. Coleman was regarded as one of the South's richest Blacks. Unlike many wealthy Blacks, he gave financial support to several organizations, especially Black colleges and universities. He contributed money to Livingstone College, and served on its Board of Trustees. He also served on the Board of Trustees of Shaw University

189

Warren Coleman

and Howard University. Coleman supported the North Carolina Orphan's Home in Oxford, Zion Hill Church, and Price Memorial Temple in Concord.

Warren C. Coleman's greatest contribution was as founder and president of the first Black-owned and operated textile company in the United States. In 1897, Coleman, with the support of Blacks and some Whites, such as Washington Duke, opened Coleman Manufacturing Company. This company sold stock to the tune of one hundred thousand dollars. Its charter prescribed its purpose:

> "...to spin, weave, manufacture, finish, and sell warps, yarns, cloth, prints, and fabric made from cotton and wool; buy and sell wood, iron, steel, tin, and other metal products; to make, manufacture, buy, and sell brick, pipe, and tile; and to mine, quarry, cut, shape, and sell all kinds of rock and stone."

Because of underfinancing and Coleman's sudden death, the company went into bankruptcy. Coleman's dream came true to a limited degree because it did show that if Blacks pooled their resources they could start a major business. He died March 31, 1904, at age fifty-five. Warren Clay Coleman was a shoemaker, property owner, churchman, businessman, manufacturer, benefactor, and entrepreneur. His marker is located on **US 601 Bypass at Main Street south of Concord, Cabarrus County.**

LINCOLNTON

HIRAM R. REVELS
—1822-1901—
First black to serve in
Congress. Native of N.C.
Mississippi   senator.
1870-1871. Operated own
barbershop here. 1840s.

Hiram Rhoades Revels was born a free Black in 1822, in Fayetteville, North Carolina. It has been stated that he may have received his early schooling from a Black woman in Fayetteville. He moved to Lincolnton, North Carolina in 1838 and operated a barbershop there until 1844 or 1845. In that year, he attended Union County Quaker Seminary and later a Black seminary in Drake County. In 1845, he became an ordained minister of the African Methodist Episcopal Church in Baltimore. Between 1845 and 1861, Revels preached and taught Blacks in several states including Indiana, Illinois, Kansas, Ohio, Kentucky, Tennessee, and Missouri. During the Civil War, he helped organize the first two Black Maryland Regiments in the Union Army, and served as chaplain to a regiment in Mississippi. After the war, Revels returned to preaching and settled in Natchez, Mississippi. In 1868, he was elected to the Natchez's Board of Aldermen.

In 1869, Revels was elected to the State Senate. On January 20, 1870, he was elected to the United States Senate to fill the vacancy left by Jefferson Davis, ex-president of the defeated Confederate States of

Hiram Revels

America. This election made him the first Black ever to sit in the United States Senate. While in the Senate, he pushed for Blacks' civil rights, but to no avail. He was successful in helping get employment for Blacks in the Baltimore Naval Yard. He supported a bill to desegregate the public schools in Washington, D.C. and served on the Education and Labor Committee and the Committee for the District of Columbia. When his term in the Senate expired, he returned to Mississippi and became president of Black Alcorn College, now Alcorn A&M College.

After leaving Alcorn in 1873, he served as Secretary of State for Mississippi. In 1876, he became editor of the Southern Christian Advocate, a religious journal. Reverend Revels subsequently returned to his home in Holly Springs and became a presiding Elder in his church. He died of a stroke on January 16, 1901, at the age of seventy-nine. Hiram Rhoades Revels was a barber, minister, teacher, United States Senator, politician, college president, and presiding elder. His marker is located on **NC 27/150 (West Main Street) in Lincolnton, Lincoln County.**

SALISBURY

On March 14, 1879, the Board of Trustees of Zion Wesley Institute obtained a charter from the state of North Carolina under the corporate title of "Zion Wesley Institute." The school held its first session in December 1879 in a rented house in Concord, North Carolina with three students and four teachers in attendance. In the fall of 1880, there were twenty-three pupils attending the institute. From the beginning, the founders wanted a college that would train ministers for the African Methodist Episcopal Zion Church, to become leaders in the church and Black community. Because of lack of financial support, the college closed before completing a full session for the 1880-1881 academic year. The school did not open again until 1882.

In the meantime, Bishops J. W. Hood and J. P. Thompson, and Reverends J. H. McFarley and Joseph C. Price were in London, England attending the Methodist Ecumenical Conference. After the conference, Price stayed in England to raise money for the Zion Wesley Institute. Price returned to the United States in the fall of

1882 with ten thousand dollars above his expenses. In the meantime, the White citizens of Salisbury offered the General Conference of the A.M.E. Zion Church one thousand dollars if it would move Zion Wesley Institute to their city. The conference agreed, and the college was moved to Salisbury. In September 1882, Joseph Charles Price was elected president of Zion Wesley Institute.

One of Price's first suggestions to the Board of Trustees was to change the name of the school to Livingstone, and they agreed. In thus naming the school, Livingstone would honor both David Livingstone, the African missionary and explorer, and his native England, the generous donor of the first ten thousand dollars to Zion Wesley Institute. This was one of the few Black colleges in the world solely owned, operated, and staffed by Black people. Over its more than one hundred year history, **Livingstone College** graduates went on to become ministers, doctors, lawyers, teachers, scientists, college presidents, and productive citizens. The college marker is located on **US 29/70 (Monroe Street) in Salisbury, Rowan County.**

Joseph Charles Price was born to a free Black woman, Emily Paulin, on February 10, 1854 in Elizabeth City, North Carolina. In order to avoid the Civil War, in 1863, his mother moved herself and her son to New Bern which was behind the federal lines. Captain Weldon, a Union Officer, employed Price as a buggy boy during this time, and Price managed to learn his alphabet. He also attended St. Cyprian Episcopal School under the control of a Boston society. Price furthered his education by enrolling in Shaw University in 1873. He had planned to study law; however, he changed his mind and attended Pennsylvania's Lincoln University in 1873. At Lincoln, Price was licensed to preach by the North Carolina Conference of the A.M.E. Zion Church.

As president of Livingstone College, Joseph C. Price raised large amounts of money for the college. He was able to acquire a number of White benefactors such as William E. Dodge, Collis P. Huntington, Stephen Ballard, Leland Stanford, and Andrew Carnegie. Besides being a college president, he was a nationally renowned and

respected leader of his people. He was president of the two leading civil rights organizations during that time: The Afro-American League and the National Protective Association. He was also Commissioner-in-Chief of the Colored Exhibit of the Southern Inter-States Immigration Association, as well as publisher of The Southland, said to be "one of the finest

Joseph Price

magazines in the South." On October 25, 1893, at 12:15 p.m., Price succumbed to Bright's disease in Salisbury. He was only thirty-nine years old. Joseph Charles Price was a minister, teacher, acknowledged orator, editor, founder and president of a college, and spokesman for his people. His marker is located on **West Monroe Street in Salisbury, Rowan County.**

PART THREE

RESTAURANTS

AND

BOOKSTORES

RESTAURANTS

CHAPEL HILL

Dips Country Kitchen is open for breakfast, lunch, and dinner. Its "House Specialties" include chicken and dumplings, roast beef, stew beef, spaghetti with meat sauce, chitterlings, baked chicken breast, smothered pork chops, vegetable plate, and house vegetable fritters. Other meals include BBQ chicken, BBQ pork ribs, BBQ beef ribs, chopped BBQ pork, sliced BBQ beef, beef livers, chicken livers, salmon cake, shrimp, country ham, and fish. A variety of vegetables are served with each meal. This restaurant selects fresh meats and vegetables daily, cooks everything from scratch, and seasons with pork or butter, and salt and pepper. Children's meals are served as well as homemade desserts, such as apple, pecan and sweet potato pies, and banana pudding. Alcoholic beverages are also served. This restaurant is *open 8:00 a.m.-10:00 p.m., Monday-Saturday; 8:00 a.m.-9:00 p.m., Sunday.* It is located at **405 Rosemary Street.** Phone (919) 942-5837.

CHARLOTTE

Golden Shrimp Seafood Restaurant has a variety of seafood meals such as shrimp, fish, oysters, scallops, and crabcakes. It also has chicken, burgers, hot dogs, sandwiches, and side orders. There are daily lunch specials (11:00 a.m. - 2:00 p.m. ONLY). The restaurant offers a catering service and Golden Shrimp on Wheels, whereby food is prepared fresh on the spot. They are open for lunch and dinner, *Monday - Thursday, 10:30 a.m. - 10:00 p.m.; Friday and Saturday, 10:30 a.m. - 1:00 a.m.* The restaurant is located **off of I-40 West at Beatties Ford Road.** (704) 399-3008 or (704) 576-3326 (mobile).

McDonald's Cafeteria is the largest and most modern Black-owned and operated restaurant in the southeastern part of the United States. This twenty year-old establishment serves a variety of meats and seafood, including pot roast, ham, baked chicken, turkey, perch, and shrimp. All of its desserts, such as banana pudding, bread pudding, cakes, apple and peach cobblers, are homemade. One of its specialties is "Soul Gratin Potatoes." There is a ninety-nine room, Best Western McDonald's Inn adjacent to the cafeteria. The cafeteria is opened for breakfast, lunch, and dinner. Its hours are *Monday through Thursday, 7:00 a.m. - 11:00 p.m.; Friday and Saturday, 7:00 a.m. - 12:00 p.m.; and Sunday, 7:00 a.m. - 8:00 p.m.* It is located **off of I-85 at Beatties Ford Road.** Phone (704) 393-8823.

The Soul Shack is open for breakfast, lunch, and dinner, and offers a variety of meats for lunch and dinner: chicken, pork chops, ham, baked spaghetti, fish, chitterlings, pig feet, and turkey wings, plus various vegetables. The Soul Shack offers daily specials. The restaurant has homemade desserts, such as apple and peach cobblers, and cakes. It also has take-out orders. Its motto is "Soul Food, Soul Flavor, Soul Style, Soul Taste." It is *open 6:00 a.m.-9:00 p.m., Monday-Saturday. Closed Sunday.* It is located **off of I-85 and Freedom Drive at 3418 Tuckaseegee Road.** Phone (704) 391-9636.

The Coffee Cup Grill is only open for breakfast and lunch. For lunch, it serves country steak, fried chicken, pig feet, meat loaf, stew meat and a variety of vegetables. It has homemade peach and cherry cobblers for desserts. It also has take-out orders. The restaurant is *open 6:00 a.m.-4:00 p.m., Monday-Friday, and 6:00 a.m.-12:00 noon on Saturday for breakfast only.* It is located **downtown off of Morehead Street at 914 Clarkson Street.** Phone (704) 377-4680.

DURHAM

The Chicken Hut is open for breakfast, lunch, and dinner. The lunch and dinner meals include chicken, BBQ, pork chops, fish fillet, oysters, scallops, and deviled crabs. Sandwiches and desserts are also served. This establishment has a cafeteria as well as take-out service. It is *open 6:00 a.m.-11:30 p.m., Monday-Thursday; 6:00 a.m.-1:00 a.m., Friday; 6:00 a.m.-12 p.m., Saturday; 11:00 a.m.-6:00 p.m., Sunday.* This business is located at **3019 Fayetteville Street.** Phone (919) 682-5697.

Dillard Barbecue House is open for breakfast, lunch, and dinner. Lunch and dinner meals include BBQ pork, chicken, pork chops, pork ribs, chitterlings, pig feet, BBQ beef, and beef ribs. A large variety of vegetables are offered as well as sandwiches. Homemade desserts include banana pudding, cobblers, bread pudding, potato pie, and cakes. Specials are also offered. This establishment has been in business for over thirty-five years and is an institution in Durham County. It is *open 8:30 a.m.-10:00 p.m., Monday-Saturday; noon-6:00 p.m., Sunday.* This business is located at **3921 Fayetteville Street.** Phone (919) 544-1587.

Morris Fish & Chicken King is open for lunch and dinner. It serves a variety of fish, including flounder, trout, croaker, shrimp, and oysters. There is also BBQ, pork chops, and chicken, as well as sandwiches. All of its desserts are made from scratch. including potato pie, coconut pie, pound cake, birthday cakes, and bread pudding. This business is presently *open 11:00 a.m.-6:00 p.m., Monday-Thursday; 11:00 a.m.-8:00 p.m., Friday-Saturday. Closed Sunday. (These are temporary hours and subject to change.)* It is located at **109 South Alston Avenue.** Phone (919) 682-3790.

FAYETTEVILLE

Sam and Moore's Restaurant serves breakfast, lunch, and dinner, offering specials as well as a Sunday buffet. Besides serving complete breakfast and lunch menus, they offer a variety of meats and seafood for dinner. Dinners include BBQ ribs, BBQ chicken, chicken-fried steak, fried pork chops, beef stew, chopped steak, beef tips, roast beef, fried catfish, shrimp, and liver and onions. The owners specialize in steak, filet mignon, shrimp, and seafood platters. Sandwiches and sandwich platters can also be ordered. A variety of homemade desserts are served, including sweet potato pie, peach and apple cobblers, apple pie, coconut pie, pound cake, layer cake, and Jello. The restaurant also caters. *Breakfast is served from 6:30 a.m. until 10:00 a.m., Monday - Thursday, and Sunday; lunch is served from 11:30 a.m. until 2:30 p.m., Monday - Thursday, and Saturday; dinner is served from 3:00 p.m. until 8:00 p.m., Monday through Saturday; Sunday buffet is served from 12:00 noon until 5:00 p.m.* The hot buffet, including dessert and beverage, is "All You Care to Eat." The restaurant is located at **2110 Murchison Road.** Phone (919) 630-0270.

GOLDSBORO

Guy Parker Bar-B-Q is open for lunch and dinner. Meals include chopped BBQ pork, BBQ chicken, liver, and BBQ ribs. Sandwiches and desserts are also served. Guy Parker's BBQ sauce is served, as well as sold by the bottle. All natural ingredients are used in this sauce. This restaurant has been in business for nearly thirty years, and the owner still cooks his BBQ the old-fashioned way, slowly over hickory wood. It is reported to be one of the best BBQ restaurants in the state. This is the only Black-owned and operated restaurant in that area of the state. This establishment is *open 10:00 a.m.-7:00 p.m., Monday-Saturday. Closed Sunday.* It is located at **319 South George Street at the corner of Elm Street.** Phone (919) 731-2941.

GREENSBORO

King's Barbecue serves not only barbecue but also Buffalo chicken wings, hot dogs, and sandwiches. Both chopped and sliced barbecue are served. Chopped barbecue is also sold by the pound. The motto of the restaurant is "Discover Real Barbecue." This establishment has been in business for over twenty years. King's serves lunch and dinner. It is *open Monday - Thursday, 11:00 a.m. - 9:30 p.m.; Friday and Saturday, 11:00 a.m. - 10:00 p.m. Closed Sunday.* It is located **off of NC 220 North, near TV Station WFMY, at 2104 Phillips Avenue.** Phone (919) 373-8805.

A & W Cafeteria is the only Black cafeteria in Guilford County. It is open for breakfast and lunch. The lunch menu includes chicken, fish, liver, pork chops, chitterlings, chicken pot pie, beef and pork ribs, beef stew, meat loaf, BBQ pig feet, and spaghetti and meat sauce.

A large selection of vegetables are offered. Homemade desserts, including cakes, pies, and cobblers are served as well as sandwiches. It also has daily specials. It is *open 7:00 a.m.-3:30 p.m., Monday-Saturday. Closed Sunday.* This establishment is located at **1905 East Market Street.** Phone (919) 275-4349.

Parker Brothers Restaurant is open for lunch and dinner. It serves chicken and seafood. The seafood includes bone fish, fillet fish, trout, popcorn shrimp, oysters, flounder, and perch. Parker Brothers also serves chicken and fish sandwiches. It offers daily specials, and has a drive-thru window. This establishment is *open 11:00 a.m.-9:00 p.m., Monday-Saturday.* It is located at **1602 East Market Street.** Phone (919) 379-1888.

Robinson's Restaurant is open for breakfast, lunch, and dinner. For dinner, it serves T-bone steak, ribeye steak, fillet of fish, pork chops, tenderloin steak, hamburger steak, jumbo shrimp, and fried chicken. A variety of vegetables are served with meals. It also offers soup and salads, sandwiches and chips, as well as homemade pies, cakes, and biscuits. It serves beer. The motto of this eating establishment is "The Home of Good Food and a Friendly Atmosphere." It is *open 6:00 a.m.-8:00 p.m., Monday-Saturday; 1:00 p.m.-6:00 p.m., Sunday.* The restaurant is located at **438 Battleground Avenue.** Phone (919) 272-6854.

GREENVILLE

Carolina Grill has been in business since 1900 and serves breakfast and lunch. It offers sandwiches as well as several specials. Its meals include chicken, fish, and steak. It also offers catering. It is *open Tuesday - Friday, 8:00 a.m. - 3:00 p.m.; Saturday, 6:30 a.m. - 3:00 p.m. Closed Sunday and Monday.* It is located at **907 Dickinson Avenue.** Phone (919) 722-1188.

KINGTOWN

Georgia's Country Kitchen is open for breakfast, lunch, and dinner. It offers a variety of meats and seafoods, including fried chicken, country ham, beef tips, chicken nuggets, smoked sausage, chitterlings, shrimp, and fish. A variety of fresh vegetables and sandwiches are also served, as well as homemade peach cobbler, pies, and cakes. This restaurant is *open 6:00 a.m.-8:00 p.m., Monday-Saturday, and 1:00 p.m.-6:00 p.m. on Sunday.* It is located **six miles from Shelby on Petty Road in the community of Kingtown.** Phone (704) 484-6945.

LEXINGTON

Nick's Chicken & Steak is open for lunch and dinner. Besides serving chicken and steak, it offers BBQ ribs, fish, chicken wings, and chicken gizzards. Daily specials are served. This eating establishment is *open 11:00 a.m. - 8:00 p.m., Tuesday-Thursday; 11:00 a.m. - 11:00 p.m., Friday-Saturday. Closed Sunday and Monday.* It is located at **the corner of Cotton Grove Road and 1001 Dixie Street.** Phone (919) 243-2099.

NEW BERN

Marjorie's Diner is open for breakfast, lunch, and an early dinner. She offers daily specials for each meal, including "Marjorie's Country Breakfast." The diner specializes in seafood, chicken, and ribs. A variety of vegetables are also served. The diner is *open seven days a week, 5:00 a.m.-5:00 p.m.* It is located at **1308 Broad Street.** Phone (919) 633-2327.

The Food Palace is open for lunch and dinner. It has specials for each meal. The restaurant, specializing in chicken, BBQ, chitterlings, fish, and liver, has the motto, "Where Good Food Reigns." *Open Monday-Saturday, 11:00 a.m.-7:00 p.m. Closed Sunday.* The establishment is located at **806 Queen Street.** Phone (919) 633-5002 or (919) 638-6387.

RALEIGH

Charleston Seafood is open for lunch and dinner. It serves a variety of seafood, including bone-in fish, flounder fillet, oysters, popcorn shrimp, whiting fillet, clams, scallops, and trout. This restaurant also serves sandwiches. *Lunch is served 11:00 a.m.-2:30 p.m., and dinner 2:30 p.m.-10:00 p.m., Monday-Thursday. They are open 11:00 a.m.-11:00 p.m., Friday and Saturday. Closed Sunday.* The business is located at **2040 New Bern Avenue in the Longview Gardens Shopping Center.** Phone (919) 832-0224.

Gillie's Restaurant, formerly a movie theater, is open for lunch only. It serves fried fish, baked chicken, BBQ chicken, BBQ beef ribs, and

BBQ pork, as well as sandwiches. It has daily specials. This business is *open 11:00 a.m.-2:30 p.m., Tuesday-Friday. Closed Saturday, Sunday, and Monday.* It is located at **126 Cabarrus Avenue.** Phone (919) 834-6606.

La Conte's Restaurant is open for lunch and dinner. Its meals include fish, chicken, wings, shrimp, chopped BBQ, pork chops, cubed steak, and chitterlings. This restaurant also serves a variety of vegetables as well as desserts and sandwiches. Daily specials are also served. It is *open 10:00 a.m.-10:00 p.m., Monday-Friday; 11:00 a.m-10:00 p.m., Saturday; 3:00 p.m.-9:00 p.m., Sunday.* This restaurant is located at **317 Tarboro Street, near St. Augustine College.** Phone (919) 832-1340.

ROCKY MOUNT

Brown's Chicken and Barbeque House serves a variety of other food besides chicken and BBQ. It offers pork ribs, steak, and chitterlings, as well as a variety of vegetables. It also has a daily special for lunch and dinner. Its hours are *Tuesday - Thursday, 11:00 a.m. - 7:00 p.m.; Friday - Sunday, 11:00 a.m. - 3:00 a.m. Closed Monday.* It is located at **1200 East Highland Avenue.** Phone (919) 442-7456.

Lincoln Park Restaurant serves chicken, BBQ pork, ribs and chitterlings as well as a variety of vegetables. It is open for breakfast, lunch, and dinner. Hours are *Monday-Tuesday, 9:00 a.m.-7:00 p.m.; Wednesday, 9:00 a.m.-8:00 p.m.; Thursday-Saturday, 9:00 a.m.-10:00 p.m. Closed Sunday.* It is located at **1000 Leggett Road.** Phone (919) 442-1375.

SALISBURY

Frankie's Chicken Shack has been in business for over fifty years. Unlike most other restaurants, Frankie's only specializes in chicken. He serves dinners and sandwiches, and has daily specials. Side orders such as fries, onion rings, slaw, and potatoes are available. Whole chickens, take-out orders, and catering are also available. The restaurant is *open for lunch and dinner, Monday-Thursday, 11:00 a.m.-12:00 p.m.; Friday-Saturday, 11:00 a.m.-2:00 a.m. Closed Sunday.* Frankie's is located **near Livingstone College at 1600 Old Wilkesboro Road.** Phone (704) 636-1390.

SHELBY

Carolina Grill is open for breakfast, lunch, and dinner. Lunch and dinner meals include chicken, beef roast, pork chops, baked ham, turkey, country style steak, and fried fish. It offers a variety of fresh, locally-grown vegetables as well as homemade cakes, cobblers, and pies for dessert. It also serves sandwiches. Specials are offered everyday. The grill is *open 8:30 a.m.-6:00 p.m., Monday-Tuesday, Thursday-Saturday. Closed Wednesday and Sunday.* This establishment is located at **523 Carolina Avenue.** Phone (704) 482-0053.

Ola's Carryout Restaurant is open for lunch and dinner. Its meals include ribs, chicken, pork chops, and seafood as well as a variety of fresh vegetables and sandwiches. Ola's serves homemade desserts, such as potato pie, banana pudding, and pound cake. The establishment is *open 11:00 a.m.-6:00 p.m., Tuesday-Saturday. Closed Sunday and Monday.* It is located at **Lincoln and Lineberger Streets.** Phone (704) 487-0727.

TARBORO

Clark's Barbeque is open for breakfast, lunch, and dinner. Besides specializing in barbeque, Clark's offers a variety of other meals, including fish, chitterlings, seafood, chicken, and ribs. Unlike many Black restaurants, this one has drive-thru window service. It is *open Monday-Wednesday, 6:00 a.m.-9:00 p.m., and Thursday-Saturday, 6:00 a.m.-10:00 p.m. Closed Sunday.* Its location is **306 South Main Street.** Phone (919) 641-0593.

WILMINGTON

Club New York Restaurant is opened for breakfast, lunch, and dinner. It specializes in chopped BBQ, seafood, pork chops, chitterlings, and pig feet. A variety of vegetables and desserts are also served, as well as sandwiches. It is *open Monday-Saturday, 6:30 a.m.-7:00 p.m. Closed Sunday.* This establishment is located at **918 Castle Street at 10th Street.** Phone (919) 762-6420.

Green's Restaurant is open for breakfast, lunch, and dinner. Green's serves beef stew, fried chicken, stew chicken, pork chops, and chitterlings for both lunch and dinner. A variety of vegetables and desserts are on the menu, as well as sandwiches. Daily specials are offered. It is *open Monday-Friday, 6:30 a.m.-7:00 p.m.; Saturday, 6:00 a.m.-3:00 p.m. Closed Sunday.* This restaurant is located at **19 South 10th Street.** Phone (919) 343-8998.

Marshall's Soul Food Restaurant is open for breakfast, lunch, and dinner. Fish and chips, BBQ ribs, chitterlings, chicken, pork chops, and clam fritters are served for both lunch and dinner. Various vegetables, as well as desserts, are served. A variety of sandwiches and daily specials are served. It is *open Monday-Saturday, 7:00 a.m.-8:00 p.m. Closed Sunday.* The restaurant is located at **604 Red Cross Street.** Phone (919) 251-1615.

Melvin's International Catering Service and Restaurant is open for lunch and dinner. It offers a variety of meals, vegetables, and desserts. The meals include pork chops, ribs, and chicken. A daily buffet is served, including Sunday. This restaurant is *open Tuesday-Sunday, 11:00 a.m.-8:00 p.m.* It is located at **803 Dawson Street at 8th Street.** Phone (919) 763-3227.

Northside Restaurant and Grocery is Wilmington's newest and most modern restaurant and cafeteria. It is open for breakfast, lunch, and dinner. Northside specializes in a variety of meals, including beef stew, chicken, ribs, ox tail, and a selection of vegetables. This establishment is *open Monday-Sunday, 7:00 a.m.-9:00 p.m.* It is located at **1001 Fourth Street at Harnett Street.** Phone (919) 251-9655.

WILSON

Grace's Seafood Market and Grill is open for lunch and dinner. Besides specializing in seafood, Grace's offers a variety of meals, including fried chicken, chopped BBQ, beef ribs, pork ribs, and chitterlings. Grace's is *open 10:00 a.m.-10:00 p.m., seven days a week.* The establishment is located at **502 Southeast Ward Street.** Phone (919) 237-0101.

WINSTON-SALEM

The Golden Egg Restaurant is open for breakfast, lunch, and dinner. Lunch and dinner meals include chicken, fish, chicken gizzards, BBQ ribs, and pork chops. Unlike many restaurants, this one bakes its meats and fish instead of frying them. Many vegetables are also served, as well as homemade desserts, such as cobblers, pies, and cakes. Different meats are offered each day as part of its daily special. Cornbread cakes are a specialty of this eating establishment. It is *open 7:00 a.m.-6:00 p.m., Monday-Saturday.* This restaurant is located at **113 New Walkertown Avenue in the Jetway Shopping Center.** Phone (919) 723-3856.

Mr. Ribb & Ms. Chick is open for breakfast, lunch, and dinner. For lunch and dinner it serves chicken, ham, BBQ pork and beef ribs, fried fish, BBQ chicken, pork chops, steaks and seafood, including shrimp, flounder, trout and porggle catfish. Broiled meats are also served. There are several types of vegetables, as well as homemade desserts, including banana pudding, bread pudding, rice pudding, cakes, and pies. Its motto is "Chicken Lickin', Rib Kissin', Barbeque Delite." The restaurant is *open 6:30 a.m.-9:00 p.m., Monday-Thursday; 6:30 a.m.-10:00 p.m., Friday; 9:00 a.m.-10:00 p.m., Saturday. Closed Sunday.* It is located at **3063 Kernersville Road near Parkview Shopping Center.** Phone (919) 784-5218.

Southern Home Cooking is open for breakfast and lunch. For lunch it offers fried chicken, pork chops, country style steak, ham, BBQ, liver and onions, ribeye steak, chitterlings, and pig feet. It has fresh-cooked vegetables as well as sandwiches. An assortment of cobblers and cakes are a specialty of the house. The meals are served cafeteria style. It is *open 6:00 a.m.-2:00 p.m., Monday-Friday. Closed Saturday and Sunday.* This restaurant is located at **the corner of Fourth Street and Patterson Avenue.** Phone (919) 721-0391.

BOOKSTORES

DURHAM

Know Book Store is the oldest Black bookstore in North Carolina. It carries new, used, and rare books, children's books, jewelry, Masonic materials, oils, incense, clothing, prints, tapes, posters, oldie-but-goodie Black records, and other specialty items. Its motto is, "Know thyself." It is *open 10:00 a.m.-8:00 p.m., Monday-Friday; 11:00 a.m.-8:00 p.m., Saturday. Closed Sunday.* The store is located at **306 South Dillard Street**. Phone (919) 682-7223.

RALEIGH

Freedom Books has a modest selection of Black books as well as newspapers, tapes, posters, jewelry, clothing, African prints, and oils. It has perhaps the largest selection of Black magazines in North Carolina, from not only the United States, but also Africa and the Caribbean. The store also carries Socialist, Islamic, and Black Muslim materials and tapes. According to the owners, they have been in business a number of years. The store is *open 11:00 a.m.-6:00 p.m., Monday-Saturday. Closed on Sunday.* It is located at **135 East Martin Street**. Phone (919) 833-5269.

WINSTON-SALEM

Special Occasions has the largest collection of Black books in the southeastern part of the United States. Besides carrying the latest books, it also has many out-of-print, reprinted, and hard-to-find Black books. There is a special section devoted to Black children's books, as well as a section on Black and general religious books. Special Occasions has cards, gifts, live and silk arrangements, plants, flowers, dish gardens, balloons, fruit baskets, wedding stationery and accessories, rental items, church supplies, robes, Bibles, hymnals, and furniture. This store has a good selection of posters, prints, and sorority and fraternity memorabilia. Special Occasions is *open Monday-Friday 10:00 a.m.-6:00 p.m., and Saturday 10:00 a.m.-5:00 p.m.* It is located **off of I-40 West at 112 Martin Luther King, Jr. Drive (near Winston-Salem State University).** (919) 724-0334.

GLOSSARY

Acroterium. An ornament erected on a pediment or on a gable of a building.

Apse. A semicircular or many-sided recess in a church, the roof of which is vaulted.

Art Decor. A modern, often streamlined style, popular in the late 1920s and 1930s featuring ornament based, in part, on abstract foliage and machine parts.

Bay. 1. An opening or division along a face of a structure; as a wall with a door and two windows is three bays wide. 2. A projection of a room, usually with windows.

Belfry Bell Tower. A room at or near the top of a tower which contains bells and their supporting members.

Boss. A raised ornament on a surface, often of metallic or other material which distinguishes it.

Bungalow. A small one-story house with low sweeping lines, usually with a broad porch covered by a front gable. The word *bungalow* and the style are derived from a seasonal shelter built in India.

Buttress. A mass of masonry, timber, or brickwork projecting from or built against a wall to give additional strength. In revival architecture, it is often used solely for decorative purposes.

Buttressed Wall. Projecting structure of masonry or wood for supporting or giving stability to a wall or building.

Capital. The top, sometimes ornamental, part of a column between the shaft and the ledge.

Cinque foil. An ornament made of five connected semi-circles or par circles.

Chamfered. A slanting or sometimes concave surface made by cutting the edges or corners equally on all sides.

Classical. Pertaining to the architecture of ancient Greece and Rome.

Classical Revival Style. Mid-nineteenth century architectural style based on Greek, Roman, or European Renaissance architecture.

Colonial. Of or having to do with the thirteen British colonies that became the United States.

Colonial Revival Style. Late nineteenth and early twentieth century revivals of architectural styles characteristic of the American colonies before the revolution, usually classical, such as Georgian and Federal but also including Dutch and Spanish.

Corbel. In masonry, a projection, or one of a series of projections, each stepped progressively farther forward with height and articulating a cornice or supporting an overhanging member.

Corinthian Order. An Athenian invention of fifth century B.C. which accented the capital and its two ranks of acanthus leaves with fern-like stems reaching out to the corners of the abacus.

Cornice. The uppermost, projecting part of an entablature, or a feature resembling it. Any projecting ornamental molding along the top of a wall, building, arch, etc.

Crenulated. Formed with square indentations with a pattern resembling crenels.

Crossettes. Decorative square offsets at the upper corners of a door, window, or mantel architrave.

Crown Molding. Any molding serving as the crowning or finishing member of a structure, as in the molding applied to the top edge of a boxed cornice.

Cupola. A dome, especially a small dome on a circular or polygonal base, crowning a roof or turret.

Cruciform. Shaped like a cross.

Denticulated. Having dentils.

Dentils. A row of small tooth-like blocks in a classical cornice.

Doric Order. Separated into two distinct types, the Greek and Roman, having a similar frieze with triglyphs and metopes and a capital with an abacus and echinus. Only the Roman order had a base; the Greek did not.

Double-Pile Variant. Any house the form of which can be derived from simple transformations of the classic double pile.

Double-Pile House. A two-story center-hall plan house, two rooms deep on either side of the hall.

Elevation. A geometrical representation of an upright, planar aspect of a building, especially of an exterior or interior wall. The vertical complement of a plan.

Entablature. A unit consisting of the architrave, frieze, and cornice of a wall.

Facade. The front of a building.

Finial. 1. An ornament on top of a roof, corner of a tower, end of a pew, etc. 2. The highest point.

Fleur-de-lis. A design used in heraldry to represent a lily.

Frame house. A house in which the form and support is made of framed timbers, whether filled in with brick or plaster, or sheathed with clapboards or shingles, as commonly found in the U.S.

Gable. The triangular upper portion of a wall to carry a pitched roof.

Gable End. An end wall with a gable.

Gable Roof. A peaked sloping roof that forms a gable at each end.

Gothic Revival Style. Nineteenth century revival of the forms and ornaments of medieval European architecture–primarily characterized by the use of the pointed arch and variations.

Greek Revival Style. Mid-nineteenth century revival forms and ornaments of ancient Greece; also decorative elements associated with the style.

Hexastyle. Having six columns in front as a temple or portico.

Hipped Roof. A roof that rises by inclined planes from all four sides of a building.

Hoodmold. A molding projecting over the hood of an arch.

Ionic Column. A classical order characterized by a capital with spiral scrolls (volutes).

Italianate Revival Style. Mid- to late-nineteenth century revival of Italian Renaissance architecture, characterized by the use of heavy brackets and moldings and arched openings.

Joist. Any horizontal beam intended primarily for the construction or support of a floor or ceiling.

Keystone. Wedge-shaped stone at the crown of an arch.

Label. A projecting molding, by the sides and over the top of an opening; a dripstone. It properly has a square form, and is characteristic of late Gothic architecture.

Lancet Window. A slender pointed-arched window.

Lath. A thin, narrow strip of wood; used in building to serve as a base for plaster walls and ceilings.

Lintel. A horizontal beam or stone bridging an opening.

Lunette. That surface at the upper part of a wall which is partly surrounded by a vault which the wall intersects. This space is often filled by a window or windows, or mural painting.

Lych Gate. The roofed gateway to a churchyard, under which the corpse is set to await the arrival of the clergy.

Mansard Roof. A four-sided roof with two slopes on each side. The lower slopes are nearly vertical and the upper slopes are nearly flat, allowing more headroom in the upper story.

Marblizing. Painted treatment on wood simulating the color and texture of marble.

Mission Revival Style. Late nineteenth and twentieth century revival of architecture of Spanish Colonial precedents, characterized by simplicity of form, round arches, stucco or plastered walls, and often towers, curvilinear gables, and balconies.

Muntin. A strip of wood separating the panes in a window. Also known as a sash bar.

Nave. The main part of a church, or that part between the side aisles and extending from the chancel or crossing to the wall of the main entrance.

Neo-Classical Revival Style. Late nineteenth and twentieth century revivals of classical styles, often combining features of ancient Renaissance, and American colonial architecture.

Newel. The principal post at the foot of a staircase.

Oculous. A member resembling or suggesting an eye; esp. a round window such is common in the west end of Continental churches, or a round opening, such as that at the crown of the dome of the Pantheon.

Order. Any of several specific styles of classical and Renaissance architecture characterized by the type of columns used.

Oriel. A large bay window projecting from a wall and supported by a corbel or bracket.

Palladian. Of, pertaining to, or designating a variety of the revived classic style, founded on the works of Andrea Palladio, an Italian architect of the sixteenth century.

Parapet. A low retaining wall at the edge of a roof, porch, or other structure.

Pediment. A triangular gable bounded on all sides by a continuous cornice, typical of classical architecture.

Pebbledash. A stucco finish in which crusted rock or pebbles are embedded in the stucco base.

Pilaster. A flat rectangular pillar, with capital and base, forming part of a wall.

Portico. A major porch, usually with a pedimented roof supported by classical columns.

Postensioned. A structural member that is compressed to impart the characteristics of a prestressed member.

Prestressed. A structural member that has been conditioned or compressed during construction to withstand its working load more effectively or with less deflection.

Queen Anne Style. Popular late nineteenth century revival of early eighteenth century English architecture, characterized by irregularity of plan and massing and a variety of textures.

Quoin. A structural member forming an outside corner or exterior angle of a building, and differentiated from the adjoining wall by size, projection, color, or texture.

Rafters. Structural timbers rising from the plate to the roof ridge.

Romanesque. Of or relating to a style of architecture developed in Italy and Western Europe between the Roman and Gothic styles and characterized by the use of the round arch and vault, substitution of piers for columns, decorative use of arcades, and profuse ornament.

Rusticated. Masonry that is beveled or rebated to make the joints conspicuous.

Sanborn Map. Maps of urban areas published periodically by the Sanborn Map Company of New York for use by insurance companies. These maps show the shape of the buildings, the type of construction, the number of stories and the occupants.

Sash. A frame in which the panes of a window are set.

Second Empire. A style of architecture developed during the second French Empire (1852-1870), characterized by symmetrical square block construction and a mansard roof covered with multi-colored slates or tinplates.

Shed Dormer. A dormer window with a horizontal eaveline.

Shed-roofed. Having a flat roof that slopes in one direction and possibly leans against another wall or building. Also called a lean-to roof.

Sill. 1. A horizontal timber, at the bottom of a frame of a wood structure, which rests on the foundation. 2. The horizontal bottom member of a window or door frame.

String course. A horizontal band in a building, forming a part of the design in some way distinguished from the rest of the work.

Stud. The principal vertical supporting elements in a wall.

Surround. The border or casing of a window or door opening.

Symmetry. A balance achieved by having an exact correspondence in size, shape, and relative position of parts on each side of a center or axis.

Tetrastyle. Having four columns in a front row, as on a portico.

Transept. The transversal part of a cruciform church which crosses at right angles to the greatest length, and between the nave and the apse or choir.

Tympanum. 1. The recessed face of a pediment within the frame made by the upper and lower cornices, being usually triangular. 2. The space within an arch and above a lintel or a subordinate arch, spanning the opening below the arch.

Victorian Style. A loose term for various styles of architecture, furniture, clothes, etc., popular during the reign of Queen Victoria (1837-1901). Architectural styles include a number of individually distinctive styles but are primarily characterized by fanciful wooden ornamentation or "gingerbread."

Voussoir. One of the wedge-shaped pieces forming an arch or vault.

Wainscotting. A wooden lining, usually paneling, of an interior wall.

Weathering. The sloping portion of a chimney stack which carries the larger dimension above. This surface is usually covered with brick laid horizontally flatwise, though in instances it is covered with clay, tile or stone.

Weatherboarding. Overlapping horizontal boards covering a timber-framed wall; these sawn boards are wedge-shaped in section, the upper edge being the thinner.

Wood Graining. Painted treatment on wood panels simulating patterns of wood grain, sometimes to the point of exotic abstraction.

INDEX